FAITH *After* FAILURE

Reconnecting With Your Destiny

Dr. Sandie Freed

Foreword by Bishop Bill Hamon

Parsons Publishing House
Your Voice Your World ™
Washington DC

Faith After Failure: Reconnecting With Your Destiny.
by Sandie Freed

Copyright © 2014 by Sandie Freed.
All rights reserved.
ISBN-13: 978-1602730557
ISBN-10: 1602730555
Library of Congress Control Number: 2014948112
Printed in the United States of America.
For World-Wide Distribution.

Parsons Publishing House
P. O. Box 488
Stafford, VA 22555 USA
www.ParsonsPublishingHouse.com
Info@ParsonsPublishingHouse.com

Cover Art: Brian Banashak

FOREWORD

S andie Freed presents many biblical truths and principles within this book. Everyone who reads this book will be greatly blessed, especially those who have a sense of failure in some areas of their lives. If you want to renew your faith and turn those obstacles into opportunities for successful living and accomplishments, then receive the truth that makes you free to be and do all that God has called you to. Everyone in life goes through difficult times, and even experiences a sense of failure. However it is not what we go through in life that determines our success or failure, but how we respond to life's challenging situations. How we respond is determined by the amount of truth we have to deal with our troublesome times. Jesus said, "You shall know the truth and the truth will make you free." This book will give you the wisdom and freedom to turn your obstacles into miracles that will transform your life into joyful and victorious living. As long as we are alive on earth we will need to have these truths and biblical principles to make it successfully to the end.

According to God's purpose Christians do not have failures but processes for learning and maturing in Christ Jesus. Apostle Paul suffered more than any other biblical character, yet he could boldly and confidently say, "I know that all that I go through is working together for my good because I love God and I am called according to His purpose. And God's predestined purpose for me is to be conformed to the image of God's Son, Jesus Christ My Lord."

I have known Dr. Sandie Freed for several decades. I have been Sandie's spiritual father and Bishop since she and her husband Mickey were ordained by Christian International Apostolic Network. They have served as members of my Board of Governors for more than twenty years. I have helped her walk through many of her life situations. I have watched Sandie go through seeming failure, but renew her faith and turn her obstacles into miracles in her body, character, life, and ministry. During my sixty years of ministry I have seen many go through similar things that Sandie has gone through and not come out victorious like she has. Christians need the truths she has learned. Sandie is not writing from just book knowledge, but these truths were forged in the furnace of the fiery trials of life. Read and receive these truths with faith and immediately incorporate them into your life. Everyone who wants to live a victorious life needs to read this book. It will definitely help you become an overcomer fulfilling your calling and destiny. God bless you Sandie for sharing your life and wisdom with the Body of Christ.

Dr. Bill Hamon
Founder, Christian International Ministries
Santa Rosa Beach, Florida

Table of Contents

1. Unlock Your Destiny by Thinking Differently!   1
2. Being Built By God   17
3. Knowing the Heart of God   37
4. Elijah—A Man Just Like Us   59
5. When the Disciples Failed   87
6. The Failure to Measure Up   109
7. When Doing Your Best is Never Enough   137
8. When All Hope Fails   155
9. The Power of Revelation   177
About the Author   193

CHAPTER 1

Unlock Your Destiny by Thinking Differently!

Are you ready to discover something that will completely change your life…for the better? This thought will change your life and launch you into fulfilling your destiny; right believing results in right living! The book you hold in your hands will connect you with your destiny and launch you into fulfillment. You are now reading a powerful tool that will empower you to discover truths in the Bible that maybe you have never known. It's time for you to break old molds, destroy wrong beliefs, and be catapulted forward with non-stop momentum! My prayer right now is that you, dear reader, give careful consideration to this first chapter. It will prove to be a strong foundation from which you will launch as you continue to read the truths which the Holy Spirit reveals to you throughout this book. Please allow it to become preparation for you to move from any sense of failure to faith in God with a divine ability to experience your destiny.

RIGHT BELIEVING RESULTS IN RIGHT LIVING!

The revelation that God desires to release to His children is rich; yet, many are in *lock-down* due to religious mindsets, doctrines of man, rituals, and other self-defeating

1

attitudes, and therefore, cannot break forth into experiencing the fullness which Christ has to offer. We will talk about *sozo* later, the Greek word for salvation, which describes *all* of this fullness that Christ died to give us. The main key to unlock this padlock of "lock-down" is for each of us to grasp the truth about righteousness. This topic will remain foundational as you read. In Chapter One, you will read that it is necessary to build your life (your spiritual temple) on the proper foundation. Many times we build upon selfish desires-even religious mindsets rather than being led by the Holy Spirit. He is the author and finisher of our faith and the Master Architect of our lives, wouldn't you agree? Unfortunately, mankind has removed Him as the architect and hired someone else or we, ourselves, took complete control only to realize we weren't created to be the Creator!

This is where I found myself when I finally came to the end of Sandie Freed: exhausted, frustrated, experienced a loss of vision, and I believed I was a complete failure. The main reason I ended up at the end of a railroad track that only led to my being completely derailed in a wilderness is because I had a faulty belief system concerning God. As you will read later in a further chapter, I always believed that God was mad at me. Therefore, I deserved to be punished. After all, guilty people deserved to be punished for their actions, right? Though I had committed no grave sin, I believed that I was a complete failure in ministry. Of course it was a lie that was a seed-plant of the enemy, but none-the-less, like Eve in the Garden, my identity in God was stolen. This is what initially caused my derailment. I had such prevailing sense of condemnation for what "I" deemed as "failure." I know now that the failure I experienced was only God's processing.

I also believed that "man" determined what true success was rather than resting in Him and His finished work at the cross. Someone who believes they can never be worthy, good enough, or able to measure up cannot find any grace to REST! People used to say, "Sandie, you need to rest in God." I would look at them as if to say Duh! Who has the time to rest? If I had learned to rest in Him I would not have been burned out and frustrated most of the time. You will read my full testimony later, but for now, know that I have walked this journey many, many times, and I believe I just now understand what it means to rest during my journey. What journey? Well, the journey where you seem to be doing great is the one I'm talking about.

In other words, everything seems to be working for you: you love God, you experience His peace, and you experience levels of breakthrough. Then-ugh! You realize you're in a storm, and you believe that somehow you caused the storm! You then begin to question your relationship with God and conclude that you are a complete mess-up and a failure. As a result, you've lost vision and don't have a clue how to access divine grace that will empower you with perseverance and victory. I truly wish I had understood the truths that I am sharing in this book...back then! The revelation of our being righteous in Christ is a truth that must be taught, re-taught and taught again. I am one of those who found the freedom that lies in understanding who we are in Christ. Now I am writing so that you, also, can cycle out of a dead-end, frustrated, and defeated lifestyle and truly experience the joy of the Lord, His grace, and His strength—not because of what you "do" for Him, but because of "who you are" *in* Him.

Understand This Right Now! You Are Righteous!

You will notice through the following chapters that we will continue to cycle back to understanding that you are righteous, now! Settle this in your spirit this very moment—you are righteous! 2 Corinthians 5:21 says this concerning that truth: "God made him who had no sin to be sin for us, so that in him we might become the *righteousness* of God" (emphasis added). You don't need to jump through any religious hoops for God to love you, bless you, or especially to forgive you.

Though this is not a book centered on forgiveness; it's important, as believers, to fully realize that no matter where our failures lie (especially if we believe we have sinned and God is mad at us), our sins are already forgiven due to the finished work of Christ. We need not linger in the outer court and believe that we must offer sacrifices and burnt offerings to **YOU CAN LOCK YOUR FAITH INTO THE VICTORY GOD HAS PROVIDED.** be accepted by God. No way! We can run straight to the throne with free access at any time because we are sons and daughters of God.

Understanding this key is the main instrument we will use to authorize us to believe and declare what God says and believes concerning our purpose and destiny in life. You already know this, but it bears repeating for impact: *if you have experienced failure in life, it is difficult to rise up again with faith to move forward.* But, precious believer, if you know who you are in Christ, you can lock your faith into the victory which He has provided for you through, what I refer to as, *faith righteousness* and *righteousness consciousness.* You will notice that I will use these words interchangeably as they mean the same. It is important that we maintain faith in the fact that we are already righteous (faith righteousness) and are conscious of our righteousness in Christ (righteousness consciousness) as we journey together. With this truth as another foundation, you will cycle into continual victory as we move from chapter to chapter.

Barriers, Blockades, and Hitting the Wall!

Let's be honest. We've all felt as if we have hit a wall at some time in life. You know- those instances when time seems to stand still—especially after a huge let down (another word for this is *failure*)? These are seasons that I describe as pressing against a barrier. A barrier is described as something that blocks passage. Is your passage to freedom, victory, and limitless living blocked? A *barrier* is also described as a blockade. *Blockades* are difficult to breach, and without strategy they are almost impossible to penetrate and break forth to the other side. Bottom line—barriers and blockades are designed to hinder your forward movement. Failure locks you down and hinders your ability to dream once more. For some, they never recover from the shame of past failure. However, past failure does not need to dictate your future! Yes, it's time to rise up and believe what God says about you!

Christ died to empower you with *sozo* which is the Greek word for "salvation," and it means so much more than simply being saved. It implies that Christ went to the cross to give us salvation, healing, deliverance, victory, provision, protection, and *all* that heaven has to offer us! Wow! If we can wrap our minds around that revelation, our minds can be changed. And, yes, that's what is needed to break through barriers and blockades that are attached to stinking thinking! What is stinking thinking? It is a false belief system concerning God, His love for us, and our righteousness. It's not because of what we do, but because of who we already are! I know that I am hammering that in a bit, but it bears repeating as our minds are being renewed to truth concerning our identity in Christ.

Living More Freely Than Religion Allows

We are in a season where mankind is realizing that a relationship with God is needed. However, relationship has been based upon humanity adhering to rituals, erroneous traditions, religious mindsets, and religious rules all in the name of "religion." In all of this, mankind has accepted a "form of religion," but has not experienced the raw power of God. These forms of religion became substitutes for our relationship with God. This, in turn, robs us of the faith needed to experience the supernatural. The apostle Paul recognized this as he addressed Timothy in 2 Timothy 3:5.

Unfortunately, the church still has a legalistic mindset. By this I mean that many are still attempting to perform for God and are still serving God with an Old Covenant mentality. The Word of God says that the law "shuts up" faith! Yes! Allow me to quote from the New American Standard Bible: "But before faith came, we kept in custody under the law, being shut up to the faith which was later to be revealed" (Galatians 3:23).

In other words, when we operate under a mindset influenced by the Law rather than God's grace, we really don't need faith! Think about it for a moment: if you have a list of rules and you follow them ritualistically why would you need your faith to be operating? After all, you fulfilled the rules in your own strength—you knew the list, the Law, the rules—so you just fulfill it without even having to talk to God about His giving you the strength to do it all! When we are led by the

Spirit of God and not rules (the Law), we have to listen to His voice and completely depend upon His grace to obey His directives. Failure often occurs because we don't ask God what He desires for our lives and, therefore, we depend upon what we already know and attempt to move forward in our own strength.

Barriers and blockades appear many times whenever we worship God through man-made doctrines. Why? Again, we don't need faith and without faith it is impossible to please God. Let's take a fresh look at why God is not pleased when we allow the Law to silence our faith. Hebrews 11:6 says, "And without faith it is impossible to please God, because anyone who comes to him must believe that he exists and that he rewards those who earnestly seek him."

For many years I felt condemned whenever I thought I had failed in some way to "have enough faith." I believed it was always *my* responsibility to somehow continually conjure up levels of faith so that I could please God and then get a breakthrough. However, when we do a Greek study on the phrase "impossible to *please* God," we realize the word "please" means that God is entirely gratified because we are "fully agreeable." What does this mean? It means this: God is pleased when we use our faith to agree with Him and all that He says concerning Himself and us! Wow! Can you see it's not about you or me doing everything "right" so that He is pleased? It's a matter of agreeing with Him which shifts our faith into action and produces desired results! Maybe we've hit blockades because we need to rest in God; if so, agree with His Word which will remove obstacles for us. I think it is

> AGREEING WITH GOD WILL CYCLE US OUT OF MANY WILDERNESS JOURNEYS.

safe to conclude that agreeing with God will cycle us out of many wilderness journeys (and bondage to the Law is definitely a wilderness experience).

If we have allowed our faith to be silenced due to our strict adherence to doctrines of man or religious tradition, we inadvertently have become self-centered rather than God-centered. And, please hear my heart concerning this: it doesn't mean that God becomes mad at you! After all, most of us are stuck doing things the same old way because we're comfortable there. God knows that about human nature. He does, however, enjoy being *pleased* with our obedience. Ready for another challenging thought? Obedience is not about adhering to the Law (doctrines, religious mindsets, etc); it is all about being led by the Spirit. When we follow the Spirit and His directives, then we are willingly obedient vessels. The Word reminds us that it is the Father's good pleasure to give us the Kingdom (Luke 12:32).

Jesus said, "But seek first the kingdom of God and His righteousness, and all these things shall be added to you" (Matthew 6:33, NKJV). The main focus in this passage is "His righteousness." When we seek our own righteousness we will always fall short. Actually, it's an impossible task. However, when we seek His righteousness it becomes so easy! This is because I am seeking what He has already done for me! It's not my personal righteousness that is important; it is His, and He offers it to all of those who are "in Him." Matthew 6:33 instructs us to "seek first His kingdom and His righteousness." Did you know that we are to "seek" not only the benefits of His kingdom, but also His righteousness? The word "seek" in the Greek is the word *zeteo* and it means to crave, desire, and worship. Believers, I believe it is clear that we are to crave His righteousness and worship Him for it! This means the Kingdom is not about our attempts to become (and remain) righteous! We have to come to the realization that what so many of us have labeled as "religion" is actually our own attempts to find God or to become holy enough or righteous enough so that God will love and accept us.

This is a false belief system concerning God. If throughout this book I can get you to change the way you think about God, the result will be that faith will rise up. How is that? Because you will understand that God is teaching you new truths concerning your *true* identity in Christ; you are in Him and already holy and righteous. With that understanding, you can continually run *to* God rather than run *from* Him due to shame. There is no more shame once you realize who you already are in Christ!

Faith Righteousness and Sin Consciousness

As I stated earlier, I will use these words *faith consciousness* and *righteousness consciousness* interchangeably through this book. They are one in the same as we maintain conscious faith in our righteousness through Christ. What He accomplished at the cross is eternal— meaning that sin and shame were destroyed at the cross once and for all.

> AGREEING WITH GOD WILL CYCLE US OUT OF MANY WILDERNESS JOURNEYS.

Now, allow me to introduce a new term that opposes each of us maintaining faith in the completed work at the cross: sin consciousness. Again, for now, have faith in the fact that you are righteous (accepted, holy, etc.) in Christ. Knowing that truth, you can cycle out of sin consciousness. Sin consciousness is all about our remaining conscious of our sins. It is all about wrong focus. We focus on our "bads": shortcomings, failures, inabilities, insecurities, shame, and condemnation. But, when we focus on faith righteousness we focus our faith on the finished work of Jesus Christ at Calvary and on His resurrection. This gives us right standing with God (which is the definition of righteousness), and we stand before Him as if we never sinned! Please understand that righteousness is a gift that cannot be earned. I know that I am hammering this point a bit, but I never want to take for granted what Christ did for us at the cross. You will read more about this as we continue to move along from chapter to chapter, but settle this in your heart now that you are righteous because of the blood of Jesus and the finished work at the cross. We are not righteous because of our religious works, our own holiness, or religious doctrines. Receive His righteousness as a gift from heaven!

At the cross, there was a divine exchange. Jesus took upon Himself our sin and gave us His righteousness. We are, therefore, in right standing with God and are upright before Him. There is nothing for us to do to be more righteous—we simply accept this as a gift through faith. Now, through this revelation we can cycle out of a mentality of failure, shame, guilt, and condemnation and live a life that is fulfilled. Remember this Scripture through our journey together: "For He (the Father) hath made Him (the Son, Jesus) to be sin for us, who knew no sin; that we might be made the righteousness of God in Him" (2 Corinthians 5:21, KJV).

Please take note that we were "made" the righteousness of God. Being "made" is a state of being; we don't have to struggle to become! Isn't that freeing? Righteousness is not about what man can attain, but simply a gift that we receive by faith. So, can you see how you can become blocked or locked down if you believe wrongly? However, knowing who you are can empower you with faith to move forward and fulfill your dreams and destiny. Dear one, you are already what Jesus made you through His finished work. Once you repent of your sins and accept His eternal gift of salvation, there is nothing more for you to do; there is not one thing more that you can do to become more righteous, more holy, or more acceptable to Him. God sees you through the blood of Jesus which makes you completely acceptable—always!

2 Corinthians 5:21 reminds us that Jesus became sin. This was not by His sin, but by our sin. The Word of God states that "while we were still sinners" (Romans 5:8, KJV), God took every sin, every wrong, and every "bad" and put it all upon His sinless Son. Jesus, in turn, became our sin—the sacrificial Lamb slain upon the cross—in order to bring us into right standing with Him which makes us righteous! Because Jesus did this for us, we are therefore free from the Law—all religion, legalism, and religious performance on our part—to gain God's love and acceptance. And, yes, we are free from the devil's lies, tactics, and seductions as Christ defeated him and put him under our feet! (Read more about our authority over demonic strongholds later).

There is no amount of self-discipline, behavior modification, or strict religious guidelines that we could ever achieve to make us more acceptable to God. Jesus paid the full price—that's it. He gave His righteousness to each of us as a gift in complete exchange for our unrighteousness. Hallelujah! This means our past sins have no more effect on our righteousness. We just need to completely stop seeing ourselves as shameful, sinful, helpless sheep. No! We are the righteous, redeemed, restored children of God!

Proper Focus

So, believer, as you continue to read, attempt to remember what Jesus, Himself, did right rather than all that you have done wrong. Doing so will press you past sin consciousness and wrong believing. Every time an emotional scar attempts to resurface, don't focus on the pain, focus on the victory you have in Christ. If you remember your sins, know that it is God's desire for you to understand and confess that the cross set you free from the effects of those sins. This means condemnation has no more place in your belief system.

It's true that if you focus on your sin, the more sin you will commit. Why? Because you become like the object of your focus. A great example of this is Jacob placing the sheep before spotted and speckled branches (see Genesis 30:37-39). If we focus on Jesus we can also be transformed into that same image!

When you are under condemnation your legalistic mindset says you must perform perfectly for God; at that time, you succumb to a type of death assignment. If you recall, the Law is called the "ministry of death." Therefore, the Law ministers death to you rather than life. If you continue to focus on your failures and your sins, you will remain miserable. It's time for all of us to focus on all that Jesus did *right* through His death, burial, and resurrection. Making this more personal again—*when you do this, the blockades and barriers have to yield to your faith.* If you put this concept into practice, you will learn to immediately challenge every negative thought yourself. He will lead you to trust in His unconditional love.

Overcoming the Blockade of Insecurity
Connected to Failure

I want to briefly discuss insecurity because it is strongly connected to an inability to gain faith after experiencing failure. In the following chapters, we will delve deeper to discuss hopelessness, grief, and despair. But for now, I believe you need to launch powerfully out of that sense of worthlessness that comes during seasons of failure. If you have been experiencing insecurity, I can almost guarantee that you have attempted to control your own life. Maybe a Jezebel spirit has had an open door to release death and witchcraft assignments against you. I discuss in chapter two how Abraham began looking for a foundation and that it was his faith in God that made him righteous. It is your faith, right now, that places you in right standing to cycle out of insecurity!

Insecurity causes us to believe that we are inferior. I'm sure you've heard the term "inferiority complex." It's noticeable to us when we see others who cower down, believe they are inadequate, and are trapped by their lack of self-esteem. However, do we see this within ourselves? Let's look at what the word *inferior* implies; it implies "less than"…but there is more…..it implies "being so overcome that we are enslaved and subdued!" Precious saint, believing we are inferior rather than a victor opens the door to a spirit of enslavement and bondage. None of us desires to be yoked with the enemy, right? I am positive that the revelation the Holy Spirit is revealing to you right now is shifting your spirit man in a positive direction. You are learning that you are accepted, not inferior, because you are righteous through Jesus Christ and His righteousness (see 2 Corinthians 5:21). Because of His divine grace—His unmerited favor—God completely and instantly accepts you when you come to Him. He is promising to remove your garments of insecurity, shame, guilt, and, yes, failure, and place back upon you new garments. You can approach His throne without any insecurity. Hebrews 4:16 says clearly that we can approach His throne of grace with boldness, "Come boldly to the throne of grace, that we may obtain mercy and find grace to help in time of need" (NKJV).

Wow! I believe if you picked up this book, you are in a time of need! Know this: He is ready to receive you now! Insecurity is no longer a blockade! In the past, maybe your weight, your job, your lack of education, your race...whatever it was...contributed to insecurity. However, Colossians 1:21b-22 declares, "Now hath he (Jesus) reconciled in the body of his flesh through death, to present you holy and unblameable and unreproveable in his sight" (KJV). Again, because of Jesus and His finished work at the cross, when God sees you, He sees you as holy, unblameable, and unreproveable.

God is leading you to fully stand on the Scripture that says that you can "do all things through Christ who strengthens" you (Philippians 4:13, KJV). *Believe* that the Lord wants you to know today that *you are not a failure; you are a victor!* Yes, you are an overcomer.

We will discuss more of these concepts along the way. We will take a look at different patriarchs in the Old Testament, but through the lens of God's grace and love. We will discover how David cycled out of his shame and condemnation and went on to have victory in battle. We will look at Jesus' disciples and, how, after times of seemingly failed attempts to experience the supernatural or understand His revelation, they moved forward, pressing past blockades, to literally change the world! You will notice that I will weave sin consciousness and faith righteousness throughout this book's entirety.

Expect now to cycle out of shame, hopelessness, fear, guilt, religious performance, insecurity, inferiority...and so much more! This book is meant for you—no doubt about it.

CHAPTER 2

Being Built By God

"For he was *looking forward* to the city with foundations, whose *architect* and *builder* is God" (Hebrews 11:10, emphasis added).

How many of us can truly say that God is the One who completely "built" our lives? Or, can testify that God alone is the architect? I believe it is safe to say that if God doesn't build the house (our lives and all that concerns us) we are at potential risk for disappointment and/or failure. Psalm 127:1 states, "Unless the LORD builds the house, its builders labor in vain." Allow me to ask a very direct question: do you think that maybe you have been the architect and builder of your house (meaning, of course, your life)? If so, the Bible is clear that you have built in vain. Don't stop reading if you answered "yes," for there is always redemption with God. Read on!

To "build in vain" means that you have been wasting your time—building out of selfish desires, personal ambition, and with a self-centered blueprint. Yes, it also means that you have been the architect in control of placing your personal designs on the blueprint. Recall what an architect does when he designs a house or building. Each room is carefully planned to scale, and the function of each room is considered and drawn to fulfill its purpose.

Interestingly, the Hebrew word for "vain" is *shav'* (pronounced shawv or shav), and it is used in the sense of something extremely evil and desolating. Other literal definitions include: moral ruin and guile. Figuratively, this word means idolatry, useless, and deceptive. With this interpretation in mind, it would appear that we could easily attempt to be God in our own lives and build our house any way we desire with a ruined result! It is not uncommon in biblical history for mankind to believe he can do a better job at running his life than God can. Thinking of Abraham again, the father of faith; Sarah and he produced an Ishmael through his union with Hagar because they thought they had a better idea than waiting for their promised seed, Isaac!

Birthing an Ishmael is an example of adding to our house out of a fleshly desire rather than waiting for God to build it as He desires. Interestingly, the name *Ishmael* is a Hebrew word meaning *to hear in an intelligent way- implying obedience.* Hmmm. Wonder what happened to Abram concerning his intelligent obedience? God specifically told Abram, later to be known as Abraham, that he would have a child with Sara, whose name was later changed to Sarah. Abram did not heed God's directive; he was not paying attention! Remember now, it was his *promised* seed. This means what was promised is "as He said." There is a weightiness in God's promise—it is as He says! What more do we need than God saying, *"It is as it is to be?"*

Yet, when we let the facts speak for themselves. We notice that not believing God is considered idolatry to Him. Ouch! Idolatry? Yes, if you will read up a few paragraphs for a quick review, you will be reminded that when we labor in vain it is also idolatry. When we think on idolatry our minds immediately go to graven images. Yet, it is much more. I have written much on idolatry and allow me to say that it is much more than bowing down to a carved wooden idol. Yes, it encompasses placing our own ideas and desires above what God desires for us. Idolatry, before God, is serious in that it opens many doors to devastation and desolation. Keep reading! It is time to grab a highlighter to highlight areas you read as the Holy Spirit tugs at your heart. Or, find a pen or pencil for underlining areas when He tenderizes your heart toward Him. You will want to go back to these areas as you journey with me. The Holy Spirit is leading and guiding. But be at peace—all heaven has to offer is waiting for you to receive as you continue to journey.

Devastated Houses

Let's study this a little more for clarification. I want you to completely understand this journey with the Holy Spirit. The Hebrew word *shav'* is also connected to the word *show'* (pronounced sho). The feminine word is *show'ah* (pronounced sho-aw') and it is an unused root word meaning "to rush over, a tempest, and by implication, devastation." Words connected to it are "desolate, desolation, destroy, destruction, storm and waste." How many of us can relate to a tempest season in our lives? How about times wasted with very little to show for it? Dear reader, when God doesn't build our house we experience some form of failure.

However, it is His desire to restore all that has been lost. In fact, you are about to enter into a season of recompense and reward! Let your faith begin to arise right now. God has had you in His heart and mind even before you were in the womb! Just as He told Jeremiah that he had a call and a destiny to fulfill, so is He also telling you.

Do you remember when God spoke to Jeremiah prophetically about his call and destiny? Take a few moments and read Jeremiah 1:4-12 with the intention of noticing God's calling for Jeremiah to be a prophet even before he was in his mother's womb and then how Jeremiah responded. Jeremiah basically argued with God as if He had made an unwise decision in His selection of ministers. Like Moses, Jeremiah reflected on his human weaknesses rather than God's strength. However, after God touched his mouth, there was a change in Jeremiah's vision where he no longer saw himself as disqualified. I can just hear some of you asking, "So what is the significance of an almond tree?" Well, an almond tree is the first tree to bloom in a new season. Therefore Jeremiah actually saw a new season shifting from disappointments into divine destiny! God affirmed Jeremiah's new vision and committed Himself to watch over it. Believer, God will do the same for you! He will watch over all of His prophetic promises concerning your future. Even if you are afraid of failing, God will continue to watch over you. Begin to "see" your future through God's eyes as Jeremiah did!

He Is the Architect

Let's delve further into the meaning of "architect" to bring more clarity. The **Merriam Webster Dictionary** defines an architect as "a person who designs buildings and advises in their construction." Synonyms used for the word "architect" are "engineer and mastermind." Wow! Have you been the mastermind of your life, or have you completely committed your life to developing the mind of Christ? To be your life's mastermind also means that you have labored in vain as you built the structure of your life. Again, this is simply another form of idolatry—an attempt to be god of your own life. The only final outcome for this is a sense of failure. For example, there might be financial gain, but deep inside of us there is a lack fulfillment and a sense of loss. Why is this? Because only God can fill a void in our house. There is not enough money, fame, or success that can build a house that would remain on the rock, having a solid foundation, when desolation and storms come our way. Anytime we build our lives upon anything besides Christ, the solid Rock, we will face impending desolation and loss.

The outcome of building and laboring in vain results in:

- ☐ Loss
- ☐ Lack
- ☐ Poverty
- ☐ Deprivation
- ☐ Barrenness
- ☐ Depression
- ☐ Anxiety
- ☐ Addictions
- ☐ Insecurity
- ☐ Poor self image
- ☐ Rejection
- ☐ Rebellion
- ☐ Confusion
- ☐ Uncompleted and unfilled dreams
- ☐ Feelings of uselessness
- ☐ Shame
- ☐ Fear
- ☐ Control
- ☐ Manipulation
- ☐ Idolatry
- ☐ Legalism
- ☐ Wasted time
- ☐ Stolen time
- ☐ Premature death
- ☐ Abandonment
- ☐ Doubt
- ☐ Unbelief

Please go back and re-read the previous list. Take a pen and check off the outcomes that might relate to you. Keep in mind that some of your family members may have suffered from some of these listed. Since these patterns and lifestyles are often noticed in your bloodline, be aware that a generational iniquitous pattern may be present in your life (more on that later). For your future reference, if one of these patterns does relate to a generational member such as a grandmother, check the box and write "grandmother," for example, beside the resulting lifestyle. Keep in mind that there is restoration coming as you identify the issues and let me walk with you into freedom!

Checking the List

Now count the number of boxes you have checked. Some of you who are reading this book may have checked all of the boxes. This is because when we control our own lives, we are never able to completely rest in God. We will strive, control, and manipulate our own lives to find ultimate peace and happiness. If you are one of those who checked every box, don't be overwhelmed. Keep in mind (always!) that the Holy Spirit is with you now and as you are reading this book. He is your teacher and He is faithful to lead you into complete freedom.

Many of you who are reading will most likely have several of these boxes checked. After all, *this book is all about having faith again because you have at one time failed in your life.* Maybe you are smack-dab in the middle of a failed marriage, failed business, or a failed ministry *right now!* If so, I'm so glad that you have picked up this book. Help is already on the way!

If you have only one box checked, please go back and re-evaluate each manifestation of when you have attempted to mastermind your life. If you have checked shame, then you will also need to check off fear and control. This is because they all cycle together. In other words, when we are ashamed, we are fearful of rejection and then attempt to control our lives by separating ourselves from relationships or challenges that we cannot manipulate. Do you see the pattern? Shame->Fear->Control? Each one of these work together in a continuous cycle until we are empowered to break completely free. And, if you have this pattern, you can easily identify that we would also need to check off from the list manipulation and rejection. Can you identify times in your life that you manipulate circumstances so that you can control the outcome? And then, along with that cycle, the fear of rejection pops up so you manipulate even more to protect yourself from being hurt (or exposed!).

Bottom line—it's not about how many boxes are checked. There is no shame here! It's all about recognizing our need for a Savior who is ready to empower us to experience complete transformation. Once we admit that we really do need a Savior, it removes us from the loop of masterminding our own lives. It is only then that our house can be fully and properly built. Let go of your control now! Let go of your fear also! Allow God to be the architect and builder of your life and your future. Let your faith begin to be focused on *His ability* to change you and not focus on your failures, ok? If you will do this, then you have already taken a very valuable "look forward" so that you *take* a "step forward."

Looking Forward

Do you realize that you did *not* choose this book by accident? It is this author's belief that you have been led by the Holy Spirit to actually *look forward* (as Abraham did) to having this book which you now hold! I believe that you have even cried out to God for an answer in prayer concerning your lack of personal breakthrough. Maybe for a very long time you were *looking forward* to a particular breakthrough in your life.

Believer, let me assure you that God is now answering your prayers. He desires to build you and to establish you in truth so that you can fully enter into a place of complete trust in Him. When God promised us a Land of Rest and a Promised Land, He was not simply referring to a piece of real estate; He was referring to Himself! He desires that we know Him, trust Him, and allow Him to build us-completely.

Now, before we get going I really need for you to listen up for a moment: you are not a failure! We never fail if we are a believer in God. We don't ever "fail;" we simply grow and learn from past experiences. Also, and we will discuss this more later, it's important for us to try to remember that we are not what we do! In other words, our identity is in Christ and not what we do for Him. Performance-oriented believers set themselves up for failure as they are focused on works, and there is connected to that a foreboding feeling that we can never measure up! Again, all performance orientation will be brought to the light as we take this journey together. However, and I am saying this because I want you to shift into a success mindset; you don't want to miss out on one single inspiration from the Lord as you read from chapter to chapter in this book. When you feel inspired, you need to act upon that inspiration. Please realize that the word "inspired" means in Spirit! Yes, it is the

Spirit of God who inspires us. In fact, when we are inspired, the Lord expects for us to act upon that inspiration.

Inspired by God

An inspiration left unheeded results in loss and failure. Maybe this is why you have a sense of failure that recycles in your life. Maybe it's because you do not understand how to respond to His inspiration. Truth is, we must act upon that time of inspiration almost immediately or it will eventually be forgotten. So, dear one, grab a highlighter, dog-ear every page of this book if necessary, because your appointed time of breakthrough is here *now*! You will desire to re-read each highlighted section and re-visit those dog-eared pages because the Holy Spirit will lead you into more deliverance and freedom. And, at the end of every chapter you will have an opportunity to reflect on what you read and be transformed due to the renewing of your mind. It will be a set-aside time of reflection, actually entitled, *"A Time of Reflection."* Precious saint, please allow me to reassure you that this is your season to experience great faith in God, so seize every moment of transformation. As you read and embrace truth, you are being transformed which means changed into His image.

Well, can you tell I am already excited for you? I could go off now in so many different directions because I want you to be immediately free and changed! But, there must be a foundation laid. And, before I get way ahead of myself, let me reiterate this one fact: you are destined to be built by God, and this book will help you get there. In Matthew 5:14, Jesus compares His disciples as a city on a hill. Dear believer, you are also a city! God desires to build strong foundations of faith in you so that you can weather every storm, slay every giant that rises up against you, and destroy every Delilah that would attempt to rob you of your strength. So when we examine Hebrews 11:10 keep in mind that when Abraham "was looking forward to a city," it was a shadow of us, as a city seeking a foundation which was also "built by God." And, that we need God as our architect in life. This is certainly something to "look forward to!"

A Close Look at Abraham

Again, Hebrews 11:10 gives us the biblical account of Abraham, our example of one who walked in faith and it describes the city with foundations Abraham sought. Let's examine the passage more thoroughly so that we get a better understanding of how God led Abraham, and what he was to look for as he sojourned the land. "For he was looking forward to the city with foundations, whose architect and builder is God. We've already discussed this to a large degree, but let's delve deeper now.

I have often pondered the previously mentioned passage (Hebrews 11:10) And, I was completely immersed in an in-depth study during a season when I believed that I had made the biggest mistake of my life. There is absolutely nothing so devastating as to experience loss and failure of some type. It's so true that no one enjoys failure especially after stepping out in faith—totally trusting in God—and then falling flat! However, over the years of experiencing seasons which appeared to testify a failure, God always turned it around and used it for good (see Romans 8:28).

Abraham is our example of someone who proved time after time his complete willingness to give up all he knew to seek a heavenly city. When God called Abraham, there was an immediate separation from all that he knew in the natural. Abraham left his home town of Ur of the Chaldees, his father's house, and his family behind and remained obedient, trusting in God's directives. Seeking a heavenly city separated Abraham from building a city for himself. He was even willing to sacrifice his son, Isaac, continuing to prove that he could and would release everything to God.

When God calls us, as He did Abraham, it requires supernatural vision. Abraham was able to believe God because He had the ability to "look" at things that his natural eyes could not see. Abraham demonstrated the walk of faith, having his sight fixed upon what is eternal rather than what is seen in the temporal. He was our Old Testament example, cited in the New Testament, of walking in faith with supernatural vision. Paul writes, "So we fix our eyes not on what is seen, but on what is unseen, since what is seen is temporary, but what is unseen is eternal" (2 Corinthians 4:18).

The Foundation of Looking Forward

Fixing our eyes upon the eternal empowers us to always *look forward*. In fact we need to consider supernatural vision as "foundational" in our city built by God. God desires to build us properly, but in order for us to remain completely faithful to His blueprint for our lives, we must continue to look forward. For example, Abraham was able to offer Isaac as a sacrifice because he looked ahead to the sacrifice of on the cross. John 8:56 confirms this as Jesus states, "Your father Abraham rejoiced to see my day; and he saw it, and was glad" (ASV).

Abraham had prophetically foreseen Jesus, as the sacrificial Lamb, who was crucified and resurrected. He understood that his own son, Isaac, was a type of the coming Messiah. If you recall, he made Isaac carry his own wood for his own sacrifice just as Jesus was forced to carry his own cross. Abraham believed God when He said that His covenant was with Isaac and that generations would be birthed from his seed. Therefore, Abraham knew that just as Jesus was raised from the dead, He would also raise Isaac from the dead (see Hebrews 11:19).

Faith is also foundational for our city to be built properly. But, true faith is not a simple principle or a "get-fixed-quick" confession. Faith is not the result of a microwave study and a week-end positive thinking seminar. Faith is more like a crock pot experience where we daily walk with God and commune with Him. Faith is never about us; it is completely about faith in Him and how much He loves us. Once we have established that understanding, then everything else falls properly into alignment. In other words, when we fully realize how much God loves us it is easy to have faith to be healed. Think about it, wouldn't you give good gifts to your children because you love them? It is the same with God concerning areas of our need.

> **FAITH IN GOD WILL ALWAYS INVOLVE HAVING SUPERNATURAL VISION.**

Faith in God will always involve having supernatural vision. He will always require that we *look forward* and trust Him. True faith will also require knowing Jesus and the power of His resurrection just as Abraham was able to do before Jesus came.

On the other hand, failure occurs when we refuse to press past difficulty or challenges to see our future that God promises. In other words, we will always fall short if we are unable to look forward. Let me explain this further.

An Unbelieving Generation

Again, Abraham was a man of faith. Scripture states that he "wavered not." I have been a believer for over four decades, and I am just now beginning to understand more fully the enormity of the sin of doubt and unbelief. I'll discuss later how I believe the church has been upside-down concerning its understanding of sin because there has been much shame attached which is not the heart of God. After all, Jesus nailed sin to the cross. But for now, let's consider for a moment the times when Jesus addressed and corrected a generation of unbelievers. Keep in mind that this author is attempting to stabilize (maybe even resurrect!) your faith in God because if you have experienced loss or failure of any type, it is difficult to move forward in God and experience His peace, rest and, yes, even success!

In Matthew 17:17 and in Mark 9:19, Jesus addresses an "unbelieving generation" when a demonized boy was brought to Him for healing. Let's talk about the word "unbelieving." It's quite obvious that it would mean "faithless," but looking further into the Greek translation we comprehend that it is also described as something or someone who is not worthy of confidence or untrustworthy. Let me be as blunt as possible to get my point across (and I can assure you that I can barely even get myself to write this!), but in all actuality when we are faithless we are concluding that Jesus Christ is completely unworthy of our trust and confidence.

Dear believer, think seriously about this one fact: without faith in Christ, there is absolutely no foundation upon which to build! If we harbor doubt and unbelief in our heart, there can be no looking forward and the result will almost inevitably be failure or loss of some type. To launch from a past failure will result in more loss because we must first have a firm launching pad which is faith and trust in God. Yet, even knowing this, we may be afraid or feel ashamed and run away from Him rather than to Him! However, if we run *to* Him rather than *away*, we once again are embraced by Him, and we can launch anew being inspired by His love. God's love causes us to be empowered, causes vision to be renewed, and opens our eyes to the truth concerning all that He is. He is love and His love never fails. Any failure we experience pales when compared to a love that *never fails*, but rather covers, protects and continues to draw us near.

Doubt and Unbelief

Hebrews 11 is the famous faith chapter in the New Testament. This chapter points back to the father of faith, Abraham, and others such as Abel, Enoch, Noah, Isaac, Jacob, Joseph, and Moses. While we are on the subject of our need to have faith in God, I believe we need to look closely at a passage I cut my faith teeth on. It is Hebrews 11:6 and it explains just how important it is for us to have faith. Go ahead and take a moment to drink this in: "And it is impossible to please God without faith. Anyone who wants to come to him must believe that God exists and that he rewards those who sincerely seek him" (NLT).

I love rewards, but the reward is not my motive. Even though Paul spoke of running the race and winning the prize, I always want my ultimate motive to first please God. The reward or the prizes for doing so are simply a by-product.

However, concerning doubt and unbelief—I have asked myself over and over this pointed question, "Why can't we, as believers, just believe?" Instead, we try to figure everything out. Somewhere deep inside ourselves we just don't trust God. Satan, the accuser of the brethren, would suggest to you that God is just like all the others who have left, betrayed, or cheated on us. A present-day example would be someone who suffered due to marriage betrayal and later attempted to trust again and remain faithful. Failure, loss, and even pain from the past will always attempt to dictate the future. And, then there is satan who is bent on speaking shameful lies concerning our failures.

Why do we listen to the lies of satan? The fear of the unknown can be an un-ending nightmare if we focus on the *what if's* and the *why's*! So often we are blinded by our own unbelief. I have heard it said many times that true visibility extends no further than about six inches from our noses! We do not always recognize we shy away from God out of our shame—never approaching Him and believing for His grace to achieve the fullness of our destiny. Another bottom line is that we simply don't trust Him to give us good things! However, the truth is this: He *is* faithful, He *is* trustworthy and He *desires* to launch us forward from a firm foundation built upon His everlasting love for us!

The Firm Foundation

There are so many scriptures that discuss the faithfulness of God and that also identify Him as a "firm" foundation upon which we can trust and stand. Psalm 18:2 is one of my favorites:

The Lord is my Rock, my Fortress, and my Deliverer; my God, my keen and firm Strength in Whom I will trust and take refuge, my Shield, and the Horn of my salvation, my High Tower" (AMP).

I pray you took some time and drank from that deep well! Look again at the attributes of the Lord as it declares the Lord is:

- my Rock
- my Fortress
- my Deliverer
- my God
- my keen and firm Strength
- in Whom I will trust and take refuge
- my Shield
- the Horn of my salvation
- my High Tower

Wow! Did you notice the capitalized words? This means that it was referring to the Lord with those as His names. In other words, when you need a fortress you would go to the Fortress (who is God!). He is the Rock—first letter capitalized—meaning the rock was not an object, but rather a Person!

Precious saint, God is raising up a new generation of believers. Yes, there is a generation of people who will be determined not to be as their forefathers, but will trust the Lord and remain loyal to Him. As we end this chapter, let's ponder on Psalm 78:8. See if you can relate to a generation who will not be like past generations who rejected God, but choose to be a part of those who trust God and are faithful to Him:

They would not be like their ancestors—a stubborn
and rebellious generation, whose hearts were not
loyal to God, whose spirits were not faithful to him.

Do you notice the word "loyal?" It is derived from the
very same Hebrew word as "firm!" Remember a few paragraphs
back when I wrote concerning someone who weathered
betrayal in marriage and was attempting to trust someone
again? Well, people who have suffered in that fashion need
someone in their lives that is solid and firm—yes, like a rock
that stabilizes them. Maybe as I am writing, I am hitting the
bull's eye concerning you and your belief
system concerning God and even yourself.
Please don't start squirming or feel ashamed
in any way. My heart is that I have made
too many messes to judge anyone. However,
there is great inspiration behind these
words being written. Yes, the Holy Spirit
has inspired me to inspire you. I have experienced much failure
first-hand. I suffered for years with addictions and eating
disorders. But, there came a time when I had to let go of my
past shame and fully embrace the Savior to completely set me
free. Dear one, I'm all about freedom; trust me, please. The
road on which we are going to journey together will expose and
identify the chains of past failures, betrayals, grief, and loss.
And, you will reconnect to the One who breaks those chains—
the one and only Bondage Breaker Himself!

> SALVATION MEANS SO MUCH MORE THAN BEING SAVED.

You are journeying another Freedom Road with Sandie
Freed. Can you hear my chuckle as I call myself Sandie-the-
Freed? I am certain that I was purposed to point the way to
Jesus Christ, the One who died at Calvary and provided *sozo*
for each of us. *Sozo* is the Greek word for "salvation" and it

means so much more than being "saved." *Sozo* provides healing, deliverance, salvation, and everything heaven has to offer! Dear reader, I want you to experience heaven, right now.

It's time to drink in the words of Christ and exchange garments of shame for garments of joy! Will you come to the well with me and meet the Well of Living Water? I know you will. I have prayed for you already! Let's now journey together—I'm excited for you to experience God's steadfast Word in a very tangible way!

A Prayer for You

Father, in the precious name of Your Son, Jesus Christ, I thank You for every reader that You led to pick up this book. Regardless of what has been experienced—whether it is failure, loss, disappointment or any type of tragedy in their lives—it is Your ultimate desire and plan to heal, restore, and deliver them. I pray that each reader would experience the fullness of *sozo* which is all that heaven has to offer them. Now Lord, I ask that You minister to them in the area of their need. Prove to them that You are truly their Rock, Strength, and Hightower. Thank You for revealing through Your Word that they can run to You in times of trouble. Father, You said that You sent Your Son, Jesus Christ, and that You healed Your children. Thank You for healing hearts and lives, right now, in Jesus' name. Amen.

A Time of Reflection

1. Being honest with yourself, truly honest, who would you say was the builder of your house (life)?

2. If it has been anyone other than God, can you now recognize the need for Him to restore and repair you? If the answer is yes, what would you identify in your life that needs His intervention? (What would you ask Him to change in your life?) (Please take your time here; you may desire to re-visit the chart and examine what you checked off).

3. Has doubt and unbelief limited your trust in Him? Describe an incident (or a few if needed) in which you allowed a breach of trust concerning God's faithfulness.

4. If you have harbored doubt and unbelief, God desires to forgive you. Repentance is simply changing your mind concerning something—maybe even about God. God does not desire to punish you for sin. His full intent is to restore you to a place from which you can fully launch. Repent and allow Him to establish a firm foundation now! (You may write your repentance below if you desire)

5. Considering the passage of Psalm 18:2, to which of the attributes of the Lord do you most relate? There is a reason why certain attributes minister to you. Most of the time it is because God has either proven that attribute or you need to realize that is truly Who He is! Take a moment and write down each one that ministers to your spirit. Remember, this time is for you. Take your time and allow the Holy Spirit to minister healing, deliverance, and love to you. You are special to Him. Take all of the special time with Him that you need.

CHAPTER 3

Knowing the Heart of God

One of my favorite biblical characters is David. I love how he wholeheartedly worshipped God as a shepherd, a giant killer, a warrior, and as a king. David knew God in such an intimate way that even when he sinned, he bounced right back with a worshipful love for His Lord.

David was, in my opinion, an example of a worshiper and a praiser; he was also the godliest king in the Old Testament—after all, he was a man after God's own heart. However, David failed as a king. It was not in his ability to rule and reign or in his role as a military strategist. King David's failure came when he committed adultery which led the sin of murder, and lies and deceit were all part of that sin package.

Like many of us, when confronted with sin we believe we have failed God, ourselves, and maybe even others. Adultery has a way of affecting multitudes—it is not just about the sin of one individual. Though sin is personal with God, the results of the sin can be widespread, as you will read in a bit as we examine the life of David, his sin, and the repercussions of that sin that led to more sin. You will also read about David's ability to run back into the arms of God when confronted with those sins.

It appears to me when I read about David that when he was confronted with his sin he felt like a failure—maybe believed that the door to his prophetic future had closed. Yet, David had the divine ability to see beyond the possibility that his sin would permanently close a door with God! I believe it is safe to say that David saw and understood the grace and mercy of God; this is something we all need when we fall short.

David's Ability to See Beyond Closed Doors

Before jumping right into David's downfall, it's important to lay a foundation concerning his faith and repentance in God. This is necessary as each of us needs to be able to bounce back quickly from any failure, run to God, and repent—all the while knowing that He is always available and ready to talk to us. Forgiveness for sin was established at the cross, but our minds and hearts need to be renewed concerning that.

David's determination to touch heaven, even after his failure, is exactly what we need today as we seek to bring heaven to earth! I can hear you asking: *"What does she mean to bring heaven to earth?"* Well, I'm so glad you asked that question. If you recall, Jesus instructed the disciples how to pray. He said, "Your will be done on earth as it is in heaven" (Matthew 6:10b, AMP). From this passage we can conclude that Jesus was instructing the disciples to pray that whatever is in heaven should be manifested on earth. Let me take you a bit further. I also believe it is important to grasp the revelation that if it is not in heaven, then it certainly doesn't belong on this earth!

Let me attempt to make a home run with this so you can run with vision. (Yes, pun intended). And, it is not all about figuring out "who's on first and what is on second!" It's not about some type of full-proof formula prayer that we have religiously stumbled upon and ended up in a large pit! It's really easy to understand the Lord's Prayer if you let go of religious and traditional mindsets. Somehow many of us have missed it along the way when we study the Lord's Prayer. Prayer without faith is powerless. In fact, it is the foundation of a religious prayer. Religion is not relationship with God. In fact, religion is a form of worship without power. We've bowed our heads and almost mindlessly quoted this familiar passage that is used in most denominations. If anyone didn't recite it properly, or didn't know it, you could almost count the raised eyebrows in the pews. So, let's attempt to keep the main thing *the main thing* which is that our citizenship is of heaven, but healing and prosperity are promised perks to that. Sickness and disease are not in heaven; therefore, it does not belong on earth. Poverty is not in heaven and, therefore, it doesn't belong on earth. I know that Jesus said that the poor will be with us always, but that is due to mindset, idolatry, and generational issues that only God Himself can resolve. For those of us who are believers of Christ Jesus, this should not be an issue because all of that was settled on the cross. He became poor so that we could be rich; He took upon Himself our infirmities so that we could receive divine healing.

That is what I believe Jesus was attempting to reveal as He taught them how to pray. Once we grasp that revelation, we, also, can begin to see on the other side of what appears closed to us now. For example, if we are suffering with disease, God desires to empower us with vision to see beyond the disease (a possible closed door) so that we lock into faith for healing. We begin to see that this disease is illegal because it is not in heaven.

The Church at Philadelphia

Think about when Jesus addressed the church at Philadelphia. He referred to Himself as, "The Holy One, the True One, He Who has the key of David, *Who opens and no one shall shut, Who shuts and no one shall open.*" (Rev 3:7b, AMP, emphasis added). I would like to suggest to you that David had a key to God's heart. After all, David was referenced in Scripture as a man after God's own heart (1 Samuel 13:14). Therefore, David knew the heart of God concerning His love for mankind. David could prophetically see beyond a door that appeared closed. In other words, David understood God's heart to bless His children, to provide all that was needed and, yes, even provide food for the hungry! This is why David pressed past the outer court and into the holy place to eat the bread meant only for the priesthood. If you recall the reference in 1 Samuel 21:1-4, David fled from Saul and arrived at Nob. He asked Abimelech for bread; yet the only bread available was the holy bread which is dedicated to God. David insisted that his men and he were both holy and hungry! The priest gave David the bread! Now, who could demand such a thing? Only a man who truly knew the heart of God!

True, this action was unlawful according to the Law, but David knew God! His love for God unlocked provision for David and also for his men. Plus, this action was a shadow of a greater provision—that being Christ, the Bread of Life, given for the salvation of all mankind. David was loved by God and he knew it! Even when David sinned, committed adultery and murder, he still knew that God loved him. Most of us would never believe we could be forgiven and shame would haunt us unnecessarily. I know this first hand, as I spent years in sack cloth and tossing ashes over my head only to finally realize that

I had already been forgiven for my own sins because of the finished work on the cross. Don't misunderstand me; I am in no way negating our need for repentance. No way! However, I am attempting to invite you into a relationship with God that David knew intimately. Even under the Law, David understood the grace and mercy of God. When we get that we can arise from any failure to faith!

Now, let me lead you in a story of David. You will read about his temptation, failure, and loss, and how he opened a door to experience life after witnessing a death. I love to read between the lines of Scripture and allow my imagination to paint a picture that leads our minds and hearts into a greater depth of revelation. Thank you for taking this journey with me as we take David's key to open a door that leads us to a greater understanding concerning the heart of God.

When Kings Go to War

Waking up after a customary late afternoon nap, David capitalized upon the cool and balmy springtime climate and strolled along the flat roof of the palace. During his stroll, he gazed at the panoramic view of Jerusalem drinking in the beauty of spring. In earlier years he had missed out on springtime while at war. Then, suddenly, as if reality somehow demanded immediate attention, the King of Israel was forced to consider his kingdom's war.

It had only been a short time since David sent Joab to lead his army in defeating the Ammonites. David battled his thoughts, "I probably should have gone with them into battle. It was a long winter, and if we don't face this battle now, we will undoubtedly face battle during the incredibly hot and sultry summer. I made the right decision to go to war now; besides Joab was anxious to lead again. The Lord promised us victory, but is that because I should be leading my army?"

Knowing there was a possibility that he may have made the wrong decision caused him to question his motives and responsibilities as king, "Well, I will lead them in the fall. Yes, that's what I'll do! Thinking back, I can't recall one single time I have not led in battle. Just because other kings decide to go to war in the spring doesn't dictate my decisions. Plus with the Syrians subdued, I'm really not needed. Why waste my energy on the Ammonites? This king deserves a rest. It should be an easy conquest for Joab."

The Genesis of a Failure

David continued to look out over the city as he considered the activities below. He heard the silversmith's hammer clanging away as he beat the hot silver into submission. He studied the women's faces as they carried their fresh vegetables from the market. He sighed deeply as he monitored the feeble men with their walking rods making their way to the city gate. He smiled softly, thinking of his youthful years while tending his father's sheep. He had not given much thought to growing old when he was young. Now that he was aging it seemed different.

Out of the corner of his eye, David noticed an unusually beautiful woman bathing. He could not keep his eyes off her. Watching her from a distance, he imagined she was already in his arms. He observed her servant holding a pitcher of water and pouring it upon her body. He observed as she lavished in her bath. His thoughts were consumed with her every movement; there was no room in his thoughts concerning war. The King escaped from the cares of his kingdom as he could only relish the idea of being alone with this beauty.

David signaled to his servant and said, "Come over here to me. I want to show you someone." The servant peered along with David from his balcony. "See the woman bathing there? Bring her to me!" The king burned deeply with passion.

Within moments the beautiful Bathsheba was standing in front of him. Yes, it was the beauty queen he had seen at an earlier time. Though he had seen her in the arms of one of his soldiers, she stood before him now! Bathsheba shyly looked away from David. Knowing it would be impossible to refuse the king anything, she drew closer as he signaled to her. David fully embraced her and within a few seconds she willingly caved in to the handsome King of Israel.

Time passed, and Bathsheba became alarmed as she realized that she was with child. Her head fell with shame as she sobbed uncontrollably. "I've got to get news to the King." Bathsheba had not been summoned to the King's quarters; she knew she must send word by a messenger who could go straight to the King with the news. She convinced herself. "I will contact someone trustworthy. I'll find Jacob who was the king's personal servant years ago."

When Jacob came to her home, she had a sealed letter in hand. Bathsheba signed deeply and as she handed the message to him, she instructed, "No one is to see this but the King!" Bathsheba sent him away at night so he would not be noticed by someone outside the court.

Jacob was the perfect choice for the task. He was undoubtedly loyal to the King and had at one time been his personal attendant and confidante. He made his way straight to the King and was welcomed by the King. "So, what brings you here? I haven't seen you since you married. I didn't know that marriage would be a full- time job for you." David laughed.

Jacob smiled. He did not know what was in the sealed letter, but he guessed it was urgent. Jacob handed David the letter.

"Hmmm. Jacob, a sealed letter? Who from?" Jacob was silent. David removed its seal and began to read. Jacob watched the king's countenance change from jovial to concern.

David began to panic; he could not control his thoughts. "I must keep this hidden. No one can know this! She is the wife of Uriah—one of my bravest and most loyal warriors. What shall I do?" David's mind continued racing. He signaled for Jacob to leave so that he could be alone with his thoughts. "I need a solution; I need a plan!" David was up all night in deep despair.

Each time David thought of a plan it was like a chess game. With every move, there was opposition standing before him needing another move for safety. Get rid of one problem and another would pop up. Yet, David finally came up with a solution. Plan A was this: He would call for Uriah to come dine with him at court. The king would ask how the war was going and then reward the loyal warrior by allowing him to sleep with his wife, (the now pregnant) Bathsheba! Then the pregnancy could easily be understood that Uriah was the true father. Right? David sighed with relief, not knowing that later a Plan B and even C would be required.

David Plans Uriah's Death

The plan was underway. When Uriah received his summon to meet with the King, he left the battle immediately and headed for court. It was nightfall when he arrived, but David noticed him from a distance, "Uriah!" My loyal warrior! Over here!" David signaled him to his table. He had rehearsed this night in his mind repeatedly. "Come, sit; dine with me." David signaled for his servants to bring food and wine for Uriah. The King embraced him and Uriah sat to eat. They ate and enjoyed the music. They clapped together and enjoyed the evening.

"Uriah, I've been thinking. I want to reward you tonight. You have been away for quite a while. I want you to go home, relax and spend some quality time with your lovely wife."

Uriah left the palace, with David thinking the problem was solved. However, David later found out that Uriah refused to go home and enjoy his wife; he stayed all night at the palace-sleeping with the servants. When David found out he called for Uriah, and said, "Uriah, what's this I hear about you not going home? I thought it was clear that I desired you to spend the night with your wife."

Uriah stood at a soldier's stance. "My King, the Ark and the armies of Israel and Judah are living in tents, and Joab and his officers are camping in the open fields. How could I go home to wine and dine and sleep with my wife? I swear I will never be guilty of acting in such a way."

David could see his plan failing. "Well, then, just stay another night," David told Uriah. "Tomorrow you can return to the army." But, Uriah still refused to go home. He remained in Jerusalem that day and also the next. So, David devised Plan B which consisted of a way to manipulate Uriah's plans. The King invited Uriah to dinner once again, and this time he got Uriah completely intoxicated. Yet, even then, Uriah refused to go home to his wife. Instead, Uriah slept at the palace entrance! Talk about a door stopper! And, it certainly was one- it stopped David completely in his tracks.

King David fretted, "What am I going to do?" He was beside himself. He had thought of every way possible to convince Uriah to sleep with Bathsheba to protect the fact that she was pregnant with the king's child. David paced the floor searching for Plan C which would guarantee that their sin would go unnoticed.

The next morning David sent a sealed letter with Uriah to deliver to Joab at the front. "Joab, I have an urgent message from the King." Uriah handed him the sealed letter. Joab read slowly, and then reread the message, "Could this be so? He argued within himself and shifted into military obedience. "Whatever is desired of our King David shall be done." Uriah had delivered his own death sentence. The instructions were clear: Uriah was to be placed where the battle was the fiercest, and Joab was to pull back so that Uriah would be killed.

How could the King betray his own conscience? A man after God's own heart should not have such evil intention. Yet, he succumbed to the seduction of evil intent to cover up his own sin. He knew that those on the front lines rarely escaped death. But, to guarantee a successful death, David instructed Joab to deliberately position Uriah for defeat. What David did not factor in was that God knew David's secret. Not only had David committed adultery, but now he was plotting murder! As we all should know about our Creator, none of us can ever hide anything from God. It doesn't matter how much we attempt to control, manipulate or conceal, God sees it all. He even knows the desires of our heart—hose hidden desires that even we don't know about.

So, it seemed that David's plan played out beautifully. As planned, Uriah was killed along with many other Israelite soldiers. Joab sent the entire battle report to David by his messenger which told of the news that Uriah, the Hittite, was dead. The messenger went to Jerusalem and gave a complete report to David. The messenger explained that as Israel chased the enemy back to the city gates, the archers on the wall shot against them. Some of the Israelite soldiers were killed, including Uriah, the Hittite.

When David heard the report he sighed as if he was concerned, but actually it was a deep sigh of relief. Thank goodness, he thought, now maybe there will be an end to this masquerade! He then turned to the messenger and instructed him to tell Joab to not be discouraged, and immediately he sent one of his own servants with a message to Bathsheba. Another sealed letter contained the words: Bathsheba, your husband, Uriah, has been killed in battle. He is honored this day for his service to the King.

Bathsheba wept. She mourned for him, yet all the while suffered tremendous guilt for her sin. She questioned her reputation now even more. Pregnant; no husband. What was she to do? She could attempt to lie about him sleeping with her, but everyone knew that Uriah refused to sleep with her while in Jerusalem. Bathsheba remained both guilt-ridden and tormented during her time of mourning. However, after the period of mourning ended, David sent for her and brought her to the palace. Upon Bathsheba's arrival, she became one of his concubines, and later gave birth to a son to which David rejoiced at the news. But, the Lord was very displeased with all that David had done.

The Rebuke from God

Precious reader, thank you for allowing me to fill in the lines a bit as I could only imagine how the dots were connected that led to the rebuke from God concerning the sins of King David. Laying this foundation allows us to understand the more human side of David. Connecting the dots of his human side helps us to understand the goodness and mercy of God. I know your minds might race forward here and recall the strict chastisement from the Lord concerning David's irresponsible posture before Him, but if you look at this story with a New Testament lens of grace, we can see how God was truly merciful to David by preserving his life. The results of this sin were pushed to the next generation; the sins of the fathers become the sins of the generations.

As a New Testament believer, as I am certain you are also, there is absolutely no doubt at all in my heart that once we repent for the sins of our fathers and the sins of generations that have been passed down, we are forgiven. At salvation we receive a new spirit, but we also notice that our flesh may still attempt to reign! This is why repentance is necessary for the transformation of the mind.

Let's pick up where we left off; we will take a look at the prophet Nathan who was sent by God to correct David. This account is not conjecture, but rather a matter of factual testimony of the biblical account of David's response toward God's rebuke and correction.

Enter Nathan, God's Prophet

Because of the great sins of David, The LORD sent Nathan, the prophet, to David. Nathan was instructed to tell David this story:

> There were two men in a certain town. One was rich, and one was poor. The rich man owned many sheep and cattle. The poor man owned nothing but a little lamb he had worked hard to buy. He raised that little lamb, and it grew up with his children. It ate from the man's own plate and drank from his cup. He cuddled it in his arms like a baby daughter. One day a guest arrived at the home of the rich man. But instead of killing a lamb from his own flocks for food, he took the poor man's lamb and killed it and served it to his guest (1 Samuel 12:1b-4, NLT).

After hearing this story, David became furious. Yes, it was a set up. God knew that David would arise with great compassion concerning this case; therefore, He sent his prophet with a story to reveal to David what was in his own heart. Yet, instead of identifying with the story, he arose and blatantly declared, "Such a man who would do such a terrible thing certainly deserves to die!" He added, "This man should also pay four lambs to the poor man for the one he stole and for having no pity."

Nathan, knowing that the story pointed directly to David, said, "You are that man!" Amazingly, Nathan went on to describe the goodness of God and how He had anointed David as king of Israel and had saved him from the power of Saul. (I love it when a prophet of God expresses the love and compassion of the One who sent him rather than represent the Lord as a harsh judge!) Nathan reminded David of the many blessings God had bestowed upon him and how he had been specifically blessed with the kingdoms of both Israel and Judah. And still, God would have given much, much more to David.

I just know that as David heard the prophet, his heart was breaking. After all, it is the goodness of God that leads us to repentance (see Romans 2:4)! 2 Samuel 12:9-10 says, "Why then, have you despised the word of the LORD and done this horrible deed? For you have murdered Uriah and stolen his wife. From this time on, the sword will be a constant threat to your family, because you have despised Me by taking Uriah's wife to be your own" (NLT).

Nathan continued to pronounce God's judgment for David's sins, "Because of what you have done, I, the LORD, will cause your own household to rebel against you. I will give your wives to another man, and he will go to bed with them in public view. You did it secretly, but I will do this to you openly in the sight of all Israel'" (2 Samuel 12:11b-12, NLT)

Imagine David's heart sinking to the point that he was completely undone. Broken. Desperate for God's presence and favor. The man after God's own heart now knew and confessed that he had sinned against the Lord. It would benefit all of us to take some quality time and read the all of Psalm 51 which was written by David after Nathan exposed his sin. Verse 17 of that Psalm says, "The sacrifices of God are a broken spirit: a broken and a contrite heart, O God, thou wilt not despise" (KJV). The prophet Nathan replied to David's confession with the most profound word from the LORD, which spoke of His divine love and grace toward David, "Yes, but the LORD has forgiven you." At that point I believe the entire passage of Psalm 51 was completely birthed. Why do I believe this? David's forgiveness was not based upon the sacrifice of animals and the Law. Ugh. Oh, am I treading on Holy ground here? I admit; it used to be one of my own sacred cows. Yet, a close study of Psalm 51:16-17 states that God did not take pleasure in burnt offerings; He takes pleasure in a broken spirit and a contrite heart! This means that God never really desired animal sacrifices or burnt offerings, but rather He sought after a man like David who had His heart. Dear ones, God wants to write His laws on our hearts! We are not subject to the Old Testament Law. Thank heaven!

David understood the heart of God. He understood forgiveness. He saw ahead to the cross and the shed blood of the ultimate sacrifice, Jesus Christ! I know. You're thinking Leviticus, Numbers, and Deuteronomy, all of those religious requirements of the law which, by the way, included burnt offerings. Yet David specifically stated that God did not desire that! How did David know that? And when did he fully get it? It began when he was a teenager. He was a shepherd and a worshipper; He knew God because He worshiped Him with all his heart.

If David walked with God and understood his true identity in God, how could David sin? Well, why do we sin? Why do we fail? None of us is immune to failure. However, we can choose to combat failure with greater faith in God's goodness—just as David wrote in Psalm 51, for example. To praise Him, especially when we have fallen short, is a true sacrificial offering! This is because the focus is not on us or our sin, but on Him and what Christ did at the cross to redeem us from all sin.

Divine Forgiveness

David, knowing his guilt probably could not contain himself and dramatically fell to his knees in utter thankfulness for forgiveness. He deserved to die, yet another profound declaration was given by Nathan: "And you won't die for this sin." Nathan looked into David's teary eyes and proclaimed that instead of dying because of this sin, his own son born of Bathsheba would pay the penalty for David's sin.

David remained on his knees in complete despair, fully realizing the price to be paid for his sin would fall upon his own child. David had failed as a king, but even more as a chosen vessel. And now, he had failed as a father. David had been a worshiper since he tended his father's flocks at a young age- now he was an adulterer and a murderer. How did his heart as a worshiper betray him and cause him to sin? We could ask ourselves the same. But, we can't stay there, and David didn't stay there. The key is that we must rise up again in faith and move forward while fully embracing God's mercy, forgiveness, and grace.

After Nathan pronounced that the child in Bathsheba's womb would die, the baby was born, but became deathly ill. David begged God to spare the child. His leaders saw David's grief and feared for his health. They beseeched David to eat, but he refused. David attempted everything within his own reach to save the child. He reached out to God in fasting, a religious requirement of the Law, but God did not honor David's self-righteousness. It is the same with each of us. Our sin cannot be covered through our long, endless prayers or fasting. Only the blood of Jesus can completely redeem us from the consequence of sin. It was on the seventh day of the child's illness that he died. The number seven is heaven's number for "completeness." The complete requirement for sin had been accomplished. The death of something birthed in the flesh required a sacrifice. This is a foreshadowing of how Christ completed the Law, requiring sacrifice for sin, and that He died in our stead to release life.

When David's advisors heard that the child had died, they were fearful to inform David of the tragedy because they believed that he would never recover from such a great loss. But, surprisingly, when David was told the baby was dead, he quickly arose from the ground, washed, put on lotions, and changed his clothes.

Amazingly, after experiencing such a deep sense of failure, David went to the tabernacle and worshiped the LORD; he then returned to the palace and ate. What? How could he do that? One day he is fasting and grieving and now he is washing and eating! What about the Law requiring a period of mourning? Seems to me that David realized nothing within him would make him righteous and nothing he could do in his own strength could cover his sin. David used the key of "David" which we, as Christians, are also blessed to utilize. It is the ability to, not only unlock doors that appear closed, but also to "see" beyond that which is shut! I believe David saw Christ's redemptive blood covering his sin and releasing His unconditional love to David.

David's advisors didn't understand their king's erratic behavior. While the child was alive, David fasted and mourned. Yet, after the baby's death, David worshiped God and began to eat once more. They questioned how David could be motivated to worship God when it seemed the time to fast, weep, pray, and mourn. In 2 Samuel 12:22-23, David replied, "I fasted and wept while the child was alive, for I said, 'Perhaps the LORD will be gracious to me and let the child live.' But why should I fast when he is dead? Can I bring him back again? I will go to him one day, but he cannot return to me" (NLT).

The Faith Kicks In!

Can you tell that I totally love this biblical account? I am still in awe of how this passage is laced with God's grace. I have specifically chosen to focus this chapter on the life of David because each of us can relate to a time when we have also sinned; yet, the goodness and grace of God manifests in such a way that all we can do is worship Him!

David's failure is another perfect example of a loving God who hates sin yet still chooses to remain in covenant with the sinner. God's grace is there for all of us, isn't it? And when we deserve punishment, He gives mercy.

To me, it's astonishing, to say the least, how David boldly stood up and confronted his advisors concerning God's character. David was going to worship even after his son died. From what did such an attitude stem? Obviously, David had an intimate relationship with God that validated his reactions. David so *knew* God that he also knew His mercy!

The Scripture continues to disclose that after this, David went to comfort Bathsheba who was now his wife. He slept with her and she later gave birth to another son named Solomon. I love the fact that Scripture says that the LORD loved Solomon. How even more merciful God was to David? Think of this tremendous sin David committed; yet, God preserved David's life and gave him another son whom God also loved! In fact, God loved the child so much that He sent word through the prophet Nathan that Solomon's "blessing" name as an infant should be Jedidiah—"beloved of the LORD."

David's Great Faith

Let me conclude this chapter with a testimony of God's faithfulness to David and his faith in God for a victory after a failure. This is a prime example of someone recovering from failure by possessing greater faith in God. While David fought his battle at home, the Israelite army was successfully ending their siege at Rabbah, the capital of Ammon. Joab sent word to David that he needed more soldiers to completely annihilate the enemy. But this time, David left with his men and led them himself to victory! David was so bold to remove the crown from the king's head and place it on his own head. He also took the enemy as slaves and plundered the entire city.

You might be asking, as I have in the past: how could David be so presumptuous after sinning against God? Well, as I stated earlier to a certain degree, I believe that after failure David relied upon His covenant relationship with God. David knew God and even if there were a more severe punishment, David's faith would be the key. Sure, there was payment due for sin, but in David's heart, more faith was needed to arise and worship God even more boldly! It's such a picture of when we know our righteousness and forgiveness is in Him that we refuse to live in the past and boldly step back into our true identity; thus, we are able to move courageously into our "assignments" forgetting what lies behind.

A relationship like this is birthed many times in the wilderness. David knew that place well as he sought refuge in just such an atmosphere. David worshiped while tending sheep, while fighting lions and bears, as well as Goliath and even after the death of a son. There is truly a faith after failure built right into our DNA.

Sometimes we may not really fail, but we "feel" that we have failed. Maybe you would consider it "falling short." However, that's really what sin is; it is falling short of our potential in God. However, we will not ever reach potential by wallowing in self-pity and condemnation. We reach potential through worship and by believing in our God-given potential.

David went on to capture Rabbah, the capital of Ammon after his great personal failure. This is significant because the city of Rabbah was undergoing a two year siege with Joab as the leader of David's army. The ark was there at the time when David summoned Uriah and was the reason that Uriah would not go home to be with his wife (see 2 Samuel 11:11). After David's downfall, he was able to rise up and continue to lead his army with confidence that God would still give him the city, as well as the spoils of war. It was his faith and trust in God's ability to continue to empower him that caused his faith to rise again. Dear reader, please allow me to point out that *Rabbah*, the name of the city which David captured after his failure, means "great." How exciting to realize that after recovering from his faith-failure, David was able to capture something *great*!

This is such an example for us to always believe that God endlessly desires our very best and He, through the promise of His covenant, will accomplish what He has said, no matter what we have done or what sin we may have committed. He loves us! Remember, according to Jeremiah 1:12, He watches over His Word to guarantee that His Word to us is fulfilled!

A Prayer for You

In closing this chapter, I want to challenge you to be like David and arise with Faith. David went forth from his failure with confidence and gained greater victory. Precious believer, activate your new level of faith at this very moment. Seize greater victory because now you truly know the heart of God for you to win and experience life and victory!

L-e-t F-a-i-t-h A-r-i-s-e!

A Time of Reflection

1.   Dear one, did you realize that you also have the same key that David had? Your faith can open closed doors; have you realized that?

2.   If you have sinned, no doubt the enemy erected a wall of shame with the intent to cause you to feel separated from God. However, if you will allow yourself to fully "see" the heart of God, you will see that closed door open before you. You might be asking, "How can I see?" Well, we know God and His heart for our lives by spending time in His Word and also through prayer. When we pray, God speaks to our hearts. The way we "see" is very closely linked to prayer. When we pray, God also "opens the eyes of our hearts" so we can therefore "see Him" as He really is.

Take your pen or pencil out and write out a prayer to God. If you feel separated from God due to a particular sin or action, write out your feelings to God. If repentance is needed, then realize God is not holding a big stick to "whack" you for doing something wrong. No way! God desires to communicate to you concerning that sin and desires that you run boldly into His arms. In that place with Him is a divine empowerment of His abundant grace to fulfill your destiny in God. See beyond what seems hidden from you—see beyond every obstacle (even a sin) that attempts to keep you from intimate fellowship with Father God. He is waiting for you.

CHAPTER 4

Elijah—A Man Just Like Us

E lijah was one of the greatest prophets who ever lived and yet the Bible states that he was a man just like us (James 5:17). In my opinion, he is a tough act to follow; maybe you have concluded the same. His life is documented in 1 Kings 17-21, 2 Kings 1-2, and he is mentioned throughout Scripture in both the Old and New Testament. A quick overview of Elijah's ministry testifies that he performed various miracles: declared drought—then rain, out ran chariots, slew false prophets, and called down fire from heaven. To many of us who desire to be used of God, Elijah's ministry can be somewhat intimidating to an average saint. Elijah's life has positively provoked multitudes of ministers, challenged most prayer warriors, and inspired all who have any level of prophetic gifting. Yet, still, God points out Elijah's humanity for a reason. I'm convinced that God's purpose in exposing Elijah's weaknesses along with his strengths is meant to encourage us. Whether we struggle with intimidation, fear of man, fear of failure, or out-right failure itself, there is hope for even the weakest in faith when we study the life of Elijah.

THIS BOOK IS WRITTEN TO EMPOWER YOU TO REGAIN FAITH & VISION AFTER TIMES OF FAILURE.

This book is one which is written to empower you and other readers to regain faith and vision after times of failure or seasons of doubt, unbelief, and hopelessness. You did not pick this book up to read it because you had your act together. No, you have had seasons of distress, failure, and possibly loss; now, you need encouragement. You are reading this book because you hope to identify with those who also believe that they have messed up in life, and then you are able to relate to their finding God again and experiencing His love, embrace, and forgiveness. Yet, let me not waste a moment or an opportunity to encourage you right now before going any further. I want you starting this chapter believing God for His best! Yes, let's pause a moment and focus on the goodness of God.

Let me say something very important that bears repeating over time: God is "*never* not" pursuing you. Think about that a moment. Let it sink in. It's true! God never leaves us; we are the ones who break fellowship. God's covenant with us is unbreakable; it is forever. His covenant with us is not based on what we do; it is completely based upon what Christ has done! So when I write on Elijah, I have to look at his life through lenses that point out his weaknesses so we can relate to his humanity. Once we examine how powerfully God used him, then carefully consider his weaknesses and, yes, potential failures, we can testify that God continued to pursue Elijah even when he was "on the run." If you recall, Elijah ran away from his post, but God met him at a cave, restored him, and sent him back with power. I love that about God; He "never not" pursues us! Now, let's study about this incredible prophet who was a man just like us.

The Beginning of His Ministry

Elijah the Tishbite shows up seemingly out of nowhere. All we know was that he was from a place called Gilead. There is very little family history that he brought with him, as we know almost nothing about his past. He was simply called Elijah the Tishbite—that was it! Yet, he came on the scene at a time when the word of the Lord was rare.

He was quite bold—maybe a little too sure of himself in this author's opinion. Why is that? Who would dare say that Elijah was a little full of himself? Could it be because he kept referring to himself by saying, "I alone am left" as if he were the only *true* prophet? There were plenty of others around as you will see in a bit. Yet, it was that certainty in God that may have empowered his ego to declare to Ahab that there would be no rain for three and one half years.

1 Kings 17:1 says, "And Elijah the Tishbite, of the inhabitants of Gilead, said to Ahab, 'As the Lord God of Israel lives, before whom I stand, there shall not be dew nor rain these years, except at my word'" (NKJV). Who told him to say that? There is no scriptural reference that says, "The word of the Lord came to Elijah saying, 'Go to Ahab and declare a three and a half year drought. Then after that time, declare that it would rain once more.'" No, we have nothing like that at all—zip info. All we read is that Elijah said it would not rain "except at my word." Could it be that he was a bit presumptuous—a little overconfident? After all, did God tell him to declare a drought or did Elijah just believe that God would automatically back him up with power?

Think a moment with me. Elijah prophesied no rain, no dew, and no moisture on the grass, "except at my word." Wow. That took guts. I don't think I could do that, but I certainly admire his boldness! My determination and confidence pales in comparison to Elijah's. Not since the days of Moses had anyone presented himself with such raw power and audacity.

Yet, after delivering the word, Elijah was on the run. You'll read later that Elijah loved to take off running— sometimes it was a good thing and other times not. The fact is that Elijah was a confronter most of the time. But when faced with great opposition, such as Jezebel, he definitely put wings to his feet and took off. This makes him human like us at times. Right? Jezebel is an intimidating spirit; most of us would run from her rather than confront. Elijah was no different.

Okay, back to Elijah confronting Ahab. After delivering a word that declared drought, Elijah was instructed by God to "Leave here, turn eastward and hide in the Kerith Ravine, east of the Jordan. You will drink from the brook, and I have ordered the ravens to feed you there" (1 Kings 17:2-4). Notice that God told Elijah to hide. In my opinion, that would indicate running. Yes, Elijah was on the run. I imagine he shot out of there like a cannon. He ran the desert marathon. We find out later that Ahab was on the hunt for Elijah, looking all over Israel for him. Where was Elijah's courage now? Maybe God knew he might falter a bit so He gave him instructions of where to hide out for a while.

Or, maybe God knew Elijah would continue to go toe-to-toe with Ahab, ask to meet prematurely with Jezebel, or just make a foolish decree which was not anointed. Either way, God provided Elijah with a hideout that doubled as a place of divine provision. After all, with no rain there would soon be no harvest and no cattle (cows have to drink or they die soon, right?); God wanted to protect Elijah from the looming mass starvation. Being obedient, Elijah went to the Kerith Ravine and stayed there. God directed the ravens to bring him bread and meat in the morning, and he drank from the brook in the evening (see 1 Kings 17:2-6). God was faithful to Elijah.

Ravens are the stingiest birds alive; I have either heard they are notorious for withholding food from their own offspring! I've known some really tight-fisted people before, so I'm grateful I have never had to depend on a bird, especially a stingy one, to provide for me. Yet, by divine order these miserly ravens would bring care-packages consisting of bread and meat twice a day to Elijah. These birds may have been in flight for quite a distance to locate such provision. Remember that due to the drought bread and meat were probably difficult to find. Being hungry themselves, the ravens may have gobbled everything up and set their internal GPS toward a land offering greater provision. Imagine their flight: the divine hand of God leading them straight to provision—probably to Ahab's table. If there was any provision in all Israel, surely it was the king and queen that had it. On their table, there were probably a few baskets of bread and maybe some prepared meat that the ravens could snatch and fly quickly away and head to the ravine.

I'm quite sure Elijah's provision wasn't something from the nearest Road Kill Diner. After all, taking food from Ahab's table would be a good backhanded reminder that it was his sin which caused the drought in the first place! Also, provision from God is never second best. It would be like God to feed Elijah from the king's table.

Have you ever thought about Elijah's "in-between" times? I am referring to the times when hunger pangs hit in between an early breakfast and a late dinner? Who really knows? Maybe the ravens had to take a break in between flights or stop along the roadside park for a little snack while Elijah awaited his dinner. I often wonder how Elijah fought back fear. There are all types of fear, but let's identify where

Elijah could have gone in his mind. First of all, he could have feared for his life. You don't deliver a word to the king as he did without the possibility of backlash. Also, even though God had promised provision, there are those waiting times between being fed and feeling deprived that doubt could arise. The enemy moves in quickly with doubt if we are not careful to guard our hearts during times of drought.

Can you identify with drought? Sure, I know Elijah was provided for by the hand of God. But remember, we are reading the testimony *after* Elijah withstood his test at the brook. He stayed there, as directed, until the brook dried up. He stayed there until God directed him elsewhere. How would we respond to such a situation? Trusting for daily provision is a true test of our trust in God, isn't it? I wonder if we could remain in such a place, waiting for a low-life bird to feed us while watching the brook dry up daily. I'd be tempted to run and find the nearest possible watering hole...maybe even kill the bird and eat it for provision! Think about it for a moment! Maybe that's why Velcro® was invented—to get me to stick to what God has planned. Either way, can you identify? Sure you can—we all can. The point is that each of us has been challenged to hold steady—keep the faith—during challenging times. Elijah was a man just like us. He probably needed Velcro®, too. How did he do it? How did he stay there at the ravine day after day watching the watermark sink lower and lower? It was plainly God's Velcro®—divine grace!

Elijah and God's Grace

Elijah was obedient. He waited for God's directives. He waited for God to speak and direct him where to go during the drought, and later, when to leave the place of provision and travel to the next. How does one do that? It's such a test of faith when you examine Elijah's situation, isn't it? In humor, I compared Elijah's stick-to-itiveness with Velcro®, but it fits. We could all invest in a roll of it—maybe buy it by the bulk during really hard times. But, realistically, how do we develop that divine obedience to follow God's directives? Dear ones, it's called grace.

Okay. I can hear some of you now saying, "Grace? God's grace is understood and measured out to the New Testament believers. Elijah didn't understand grace as an Old Testament prophet!" Well, precious believer, this author's response: not so! As New Testament believers, we can look at the Old Testament with lenses of God's incredible grace! God was not a God of grace only in the New Testament! And, dear ones, He has never been a schizophrenic God. By that I mean that He never referred to Himself as "God the Punisher" nor is He known in either testament as the "God of Lack." No way! He identifies Himself throughout Scripture with many different names, two of which are *Jehovah Jireh*, meaning Jehovah will provide, (see Genesis 22:14) and *Jehovah Rapha*, the God that heals (see Exodus 15:26). He cannot nullify who He says that He is; He also cannot present Himself to us in any way other than His divine nature.

Even though there are times that we pray for the sick and they do not recover from an illness, this does not mean that God is not our healer. He is still *Jehovah Rapha*, our healer, and cannot be anyone other than that. Elijah knew God. He obeyed God; therefore, provision was given to sustain Elijah for a season until further direction was given. At the brook, *Jehovah Jireh* revealed His divine nature to Elijah. Elijah did not experience lack. The empowering nature of God's grace directed Elijah, sustained Elijah, and endued Elijah with great power and demonstration.

God's grace is available to each of us today, just as it was there for Elijah. It may seem as if I am side-tracking a bit, but hang in there with me. Elijah was a man just like us; therefore, he experienced grace just as we experience it today. God promises to lead us, provide for us, heal us, and protect us-just as he did for Elijah. He never desired to destroy mankind; it was mankind that chose other gods and walked in disobedience. God never removed Himself from man; it was man who moved away from God. Elijah chose God; God used Elijah. It's as simple as that. The grace of God empowers us to remain obedient. We cannot remain obedient in our own strength. If you've tried to fulfill God's plan for your life in your own strength, like I have, you realize I'm right.

Obedience through Grace

Elijah drew his strength from God's directives. It was not Elijah's idea to hide out at Kerith Ravine. If you recall, God told Elijah to go there and hide after declaring a drought. Again, we don't actually read that God, Himself, instructed Elijah to declare a drought; however, we assume that He did. At any rate, divine grace kicked in when Elijah needed to run and hide.

I often wonder if Elijah had wished that he never said anything to provoke Ahab and Jezebel. After all, as you will read a little later, Jezebel sought to kill him after the showdown at Mt. Carmel. I know that I have said some rather startling statements that later I wished I had placed a watch over my mouth! Yep. I messed up. I have felt like a failure wanting to run away and lick my wounds. Yet, God has always been faithful to continue to direct me even when I mess up. After a seeming failure, I have to lock back into my faith in God—not faith in myself! There is always divine grace to empower us to remain obedient. Many believe that grace is limited to having "unmerited favor." Though favor is part of walking in His grace, it's only a small part of what grace is all about. Grace involves a supernatural ability, a divine enablement to fulfill God's plan for your life. We walk by faith, yes, but it's His grace that empowers us to walk!

God's grace was available to Elijah at the brook where he drank and was supernaturally fed by ravens. But, there came a day when the brook dried up: "Some time later the brook dried up because there had been no rain in the land. Then the word of the LORD came to him: 'Go at once to Zarephath of Sidon and stay there. I have directed a widow in that place to supply you with food'" (1 Kings 17:7-9).

We don't know exactly how long Elijah stayed at the Ravine. I thought awhile about how long it would take a brook to dry up. I suppose it would depend on the size of the brook. One might compare it to a certain type of provision. Maybe you have grace to remain at a particular job for a year or two and then your brook dries up. What would you do then? Like during a time of testing, will we remain at a particular spot until God says leave? I have realized God is always faithful to speak and lead. Though there are times when He appears silent, there is always a breakthrough day when He will speak clearly concerning your next place of provision. I'm sure Elijah watched that brook daily evaporating in the intense heat and drought; yet, God was silent. Then, suddenly in the blink of an eye, God spoke where to go next. I love God's suddenlies, don't you?

But wait. I can only imagine Elijah's relief to hear where to go next. Like me, he was wondering where his next meal might come from. Then God told Elijah that there was a widow in Zarephath of Sidon who would supply him with food.

Elijah's mind must have run amuck. First of all, Zarephath of Sidon was Jezebel's territory; she was born there! It could appear that God was sending this fiery prophet right into the lion's den. After all, he was supposed to be running away from Ahab, not smack-dab into the camp of the enemy! It doesn't make sense. God sometimes doesn't make sense at all to our natural minds. And a widow? Hmmm...maybe if she was wealthy. But how many widows were wealthy? Maybe it was the way God said it to Elijah all in a type of run on sentence. It may have been easier to swallow if He said "Don't worry, Elijah. I have divine provision for you there. I know it's at Zarephath. But, there is no need to be concerned. Jezebel won't bother you. And there is a widow that I have hand-picked to care for you."

QUESTIONS AFTER GOD GIVES DIRECTIVES WILL STEAL OUR OBEDIENCE.

In the flesh, my thoughts would have been, "A widow? God, ravens might do better for me again. Are you sure—a widow? Now this is a stretch of faith. There is a severe drought there also. Where will her provision come from and how long will it last?" Questions after God gives directives will steal our obedience. Questions will cause us to remain at a dry brook. Questions will water down faith. Questions oppose God's grace. Yet, it appears as if Elijah took off once again and headed to Zarephath in God's grace.

The Widow at Zarephath

I'm sure you know this amazing story about how the widow only had enough food for one more meal. When Elijah approached her, she was gathering sticks for a fire to cook the last supper—a final meal for her and her only son. Her plans were to eat and die with no plans of entertaining—especially not a stranger. There was only enough meal for mother and son—no one else. Yet, Elijah commanded her to bring him some water and bake him a cake first before she fed herself and her son.

The nerve! How dare he? I imagine the widow's eyebrows almost arching completely off her forehead! I'm quite sure she had to have jerked into a defensive posture—maybe even offensive and ready to kill! Either position would be understandable considering her circumstances.

Elijah was not being presumptuous. His boldness was a knee-jerk response to God's direction. After all, God said He would provide through the widow. God was the provider; the widow was the vessel. Elijah banked on God's promise, not the widow. Elijah took God at His Word and commanded to be fed. Amazingly, the widow's provision was multiplied, and she was used by the hand of God to sustain Elijah and her family. Wow!

The widow housed Elijah. It was another hide-out. Elijah was a fugitive in "Jezebel Land," yet God kept him safe and proved once more to be *Jehovah Jireh* as He promised. God used this fugitive to raise the widow's dead son. His stay there proved to be a blessing to the widow. **This demonstrates that wherever God directs us, He means to use us at that place and time to bless others.** We may not understand why we are sent to a certain place for provision, but we can always use that season to be a blessing to others and demonstrate God's goodness and love. Elijah did that, and we can do the same.

Grace will empower us to be God's instruments on earth to demonstrate His glory.

Elijah's Next Move

> After a long time, in the third year, the word of the LORD came to Elijah: "Go and present yourself to Ahab, and I will send rain on the land." So Elijah went to present himself to Ahab (1 Kings 18:1-2).

Elijah was in hiding for a "long time." A long time can be any length of time when you are a fugitive. A long time to me can be several weeks, a month, or a year. But, three years of not hearing from God? That is an eternity. If I were in Elijah's shoes, the Scripture might have read differently. It would have said something like, "After what seemed like an eternity, the word of the LORD FINALLY came!" But for Elijah, his long time was in the third year after he declared drought. While in hiding I believe I can safely say that even to Elijah three years was definitely a long time! However, God's directives came, and God instructed him to present himself to Ahab. Then, God told Elijah that after he met with Ahab, He would then send rain.

Once again, I am reading between the lines. Think about it. Elijah has to meet with Ahab before God sends rain. Yikes! In the natural, only a complete fool would consider this. One would believe they had misunderstood God's directives. I'd be saying, "Do what? Go see who? You want me to do this before You send rain? Are you sure, God?"

In the book of Acts, we notice the same type of response from Ananias when he was instructed to lay hands upon Saul who was persecuting Christians. Since Ananias was a follower of Christ, he was no doubt hesitant to approach Saul on any account. Yet, Ananias was obedient. Thank God he was! Saul later became known as Paul, the apostle who wrote close to half of the entire New Testament. The once blind Saul became the Paul who preached to the spiritually blind and ignited a revival wherever he went. The only exception was his encounter with a "Greek-thinking" stronghold at Mars Hill.

Now you see that questioning God is not uncommon. The problem is that we cannot allow the question to dominate and nullify our obedience to God's directives. To do so would be to abort destiny. Elijah may have been tempted to question— though it is not documented. However, if we read a little further we notice the same major character flaw rising up again in Elijah. Keep reading! You are really going to be able to identify with the rest of this chapter!

I Alone Am Left!

Yep. Elijah said it. He really thought that he was the only prophet in the land. How prideful. How presumptuous. Think about it. Elijah headed out to meet with King Ahab and ran into Obadiah. Obadiah was the person who was in charge of Ahab's castle, and when Jezebel was killing the prophets of God, he was hiding one hundred prophets in caves. How courageous he was to deliberately carry on God's business while sleeping in the house of the enemy.

Upon meeting Elijah, Obadiah explained that he had hidden one hundred of God's prophets in two caves—fifty in each. But, I don't think that Elijah was listening well. In fact, he acted as if he wasn't the least bit concerned about Obadiah risking his own life to save the other prophets. This may be because Elijah believed he was truly the only true prophet! This attitude becomes a slippery slope for God's prophets. Pride attaches itself to us all if we allow it. I have always said that **if you ask the devil to dinner he will bring a suitcase; he plans to stay awhile.** Pride will rule and reign in your life if allowed. Like sin, it will take you places your character cannot keep you. It certainly did that to Elijah. His character flaw was addressed by God at a later time. For now, the Lord used his attitude for His advantage, and God will do the same for us. That very thing about which we are prideful will eventually be tried in God's fire. Until it is, He will allow it to fuel us to present His glory. But, like Elijah, we'll find ourselves running on our own fuel a bit too long—at least until God summons us out of our cave. We all end up in our cave at one time or another.

Okay, back to Obadiah. Obadiah was a faithful servant of God, yet he goes unrecognized by Elijah. Nonetheless, it is an important encounter because Elijah instructs Obadiah to tell Ahab to meet with him. This meeting was the build-up to Elijah's confrontation with the prophets of Baal at Mt. Carmel. All of this would result in God releasing rain again. It was also leading to a showdown between Elijah and Jezebel.

When Elijah and Ahab finally meet there had still been no rain. Remember, Elijah is to meet with Ahab before the rain, per God's instructions.

No one can say that Elijah was not a determined prophet! Sure, it was raw pride in action, but, as I said earlier, God used Elijah's pride for His own advantage. Again, let me explain. Elijah believed he was indestructible and highly favored by God. After all, who else would approach the evil king face-to-face after prophesying a drought? Only someone full of himself—Elijah, a man like us!

You know the conclusion of the confrontation at Mt. Carmel, I'm sure. It would benefit you to read the passage yourself in 1 Kings 18:20-33 for the full details of the encounter and then the release of rain. I discuss in great detail the encounter in my book, ***Breaking the Threefold Demonic Cord: How to Discern and Defeat the Lies of Jezebel, Athaliah and Delilah*** (Chosen Books, 2008).

What I would like for you to focus on is 1 Kings 18:22, "Then Elijah said to them, 'I am the only one of the LORD's prophets left, but Baal has four hundred and fifty prophets.'" This is where Elijah exposed his heart and his pride! Elijah said to the people, "I am the only one of the LORD's prophets." I wonder if Obadiah was there. If he were, I'm sure he cringed. It makes me cringe that so many of God's vessels have the same attitude. If we would only remember that satan is the king of pride, maybe we wouldn't agree with that type of attitude and behavior. But Elijah laid it all out there. What did God do about it? He used it for His glory!

Prideful Elijah wouldn't settle for one bucket of water. Oh no, he used three to soak down the wood and sacrifices to God. He boldly called down fire from heaven, and God answered with His holy fire! What a demonstration. Who else but Elijah could be so bold and fearless? Yet, he was a man, just like us!

Elijah then slew the four hundred fifty false prophets. And finally, God answered with heaven's rain and Elijah outran Ahab's chariot to Jezreel. Whew-what a day for Elijah! If he had cheerleaders, they'd have been totally worn out! It was Elijah's day to shine. Not many shine in a rain storm or amongst the dark clouds, but Elijah certainly did.

But he didn't shine for long—maybe less than twelve hours. Why? Jezebel used the rain to rain on Elijah's parade. This confrontation that occurred on the day after the Mt. Carmel showdown sent Elijah running again, *but in the wrong direction*. This time it was not instruction from God; it was Elijah's fear of Jezebel.

The Failure, the Downfall, and the Empowerment

We are at that place where we will examine Elijah's failure. I know it seems as if I'm chasing rabbits, but trust me, this preparation is needed for your hearts to be tendered toward God, His grace, and especially His mercy as He empowers us after our failures. If you keep reading, you will later read how to be free from religious performance which even challenged Elijah. God knows our flesh is weak. He also knows that we will experience disappointments and failures. Yet, He is always faithful to empower us through it and use it for His glory.

The man of the hour—full of demonstration and power—received a word from Jezebel through an evil messenger: "So Jezebel sent a messenger to Elijah to say, 'May the gods deal with me, be it ever so severely, if by this time tomorrow I do not make your life like that of one of them'" (1 Kings 19:2). Jezebel was declaring that Elijah would soon be just as dead as the dead false prophets which he had previously slain.

Scripture states that after hearing the evil message, Elijah took off running in fear. Think about it. Elijah had just encountered all the false prophets the day before, called down fire from heaven, prayed for rain, and outran Ahab's chariot. Now a woman—I know she may have been an evil queen, but come on, Elijah—get a grip! You're going to allow one woman to send you on a desert detour?

Yes, Jezebel sent a message threatening to kill him. I'm not there at the time and I am certainly not Elijah (though he was a man like us), but I think maybe I could have responded differently. At least I'd like to think so. After all, one woman's evil threats compared to four hundred fifty false prophets the day before? Would that make me run away? I'd have to believe that God would ask me to stay and now confront her!

But, something was happening inside of Elijah— something different. Before, he had seen himself as powerful, the only one left that God might use. But now, an invading thought was burrowing its way into Elijah's self-image. Little by little Elijah's pride was melting; God was even using the enemy to tender Elijah's heart concerning His sovereignty. No, his pride didn't completely leave him yet—as you will read in a few paragraphs. Elijah still felt he was a loner prophet, but the fear that sent him on a camping trip proved that his self- image was deteriorating.

In fact, if you read from the King James Version, it states Elijah's response somewhat differently. Let's examine a few verses. Pay attention to the *italicized words*:

> And, Ahab told Jezebel all that Elijah had done, and
> withal how he had slain all the prophets with the

sword. Then Jezebel sent a messenger unto Elijah, saying, So let the gods do to me, and more also, if I make not thy life as the life of one of them by to morrow about this time. *And when he saw* that, he arose, and went for his life, and came to Beersheba, which belongeth to Judah, and left his servant there. But he himself went a day's journey into the wilderness, and came and sat down under a juniper tree: and he requested for himself that he might die; and said, It is enough; now, O LORD, take away my life; for I am not better than my fathers (1 Kings 19:1-4, KJV, emphasis added).

Did you notice the italicized words "when he saw that"? What did Elijah see that caused him to run? Obviously, it wasn't good. Let me be really clear about this: there is power in words. Failure is on the brink of negative and destructive words waiting to be delivered into our atmosphere. Let me remind you about the atmosphere in heaven. Heaven hosts an atmosphere of peace. The air we inhale on earth in the natural has nitrogen, oxygen, argon, carbon dioxide, and other gases. But, in heaven the "oxygen" is complete peace. Anything—whether an old memory, a false belief, or an evil spirit—that robs us of peace is absolutely not from heaven. Don't breathe in its air! It will send you sprinting in the wrong direction! It will derail you, deflate your passion, and falsify or negate your true identity. Elijah lost his identity. Don't lose yours.

Yet, God used all of this to bring Elijah to the end of himself. As you continue to read, you will realize that God is after the "self" in all of us. Elijah lost confidence in himself, and it needed to happen. It needs to happen to us. Self is a subject that adversely affects us. In fact, it leads us to the end of ourselves. We'll revisit that subject a little later as we realize more and more that we cannot depend on self for our right standing with God. Elijah found out he was standing in his own strength. Hopefully, we can find ourselves in this example and learn to completely depend upon the finished work of Christ by realizing that our identity lies in the fact that we are holy, righteous, and acceptable to God because of the cross.

Okay, back to the evil messenger. The evil messenger's words lodged in Elijah's mind and spirit, and he imagined Jezebel killing him! Yes, he saw himself dead. Goodness, what one's imagination can do. When Elijah gave Jezebel's words a place in his imagination, he ran! That is a completely different attitude of Elijah that we have seen up until now, isn't it? Is this the same man who boldly declared a drought to Ahab's face? Is this the prophet that truly believed that he was the only anointed and chosen prophet left? Now Ahab's wife, Jezebel, threatened him, and he saw himself as defeated. Hmmm...again! This is worth scratching our heads over. After all, who wants to repeat Elijah's mistake or failure? Our failure might be something like missing God's plan for our lives.

Let's look further into what Elijah's responses were. Maybe you can identify with these:

> And as he lay and slept under a juniper tree, behold, then an angel touched him, and said unto him, Arise and eat. And he looked, and, behold, there was a cake baken on the coals, and a cruse of water at his head. And he did eat and drink, and laid him down again. And the angel of the LORD came again the second time, and touched him, and said, Arise and eat; because the journey is too great for thee. And he arose, and did eat and drink, and went in the

strength of that meat forty days and forty nights unto Horeb the mount of God. And he came thither unto a cave, and lodged there; and, behold, the word of the LORD came to him, and he said unto him, What doest thou here, Elijah? *And he said, I have been very jealous for the LORD God of hosts: for the children of Israel have forsaken thy covenant, thrown down thine altars, and slain thy prophets with the sword; and I, even I only, am left; and they seek my life, to take it away.* And he said, Go forth, and stand upon the mount before the LORD. And, behold, the LORD passed by, and a great and strong wind rent the mountains, and brake in pieces the rocks before the LORD; but the LORD was not in the wind: and after the wind an earthquake; but the LORD was not in the earthquake: And after the earthquake a fire; but the LORD was not in the fire: and after the fire a still small voice.

And it was so, when Elijah heard it, that he wrapped his face in his mantle, and went out, and stood in the entering in of the cave. And, behold, there came a voice unto him, and said, What doest thou here, Elijah? *And he said, I have been very jealous for the LORD God of hosts: because the children of Israel have forsaken thy covenant, thrown down thine altars, and slain thy prophets with the sword; and I, even I only, am left; and they seek my life, to take it away.* And the LORD said unto him, Go, return on thy way to the wilderness of Damascus: and when thou comest, anoint Hazael to be king over Syria: And Jehu the son of Nimshi shalt thou anoint to be king over Israel: and Elisha the son of Shaphat of Abel-meholah shalt thou anoint to be prophet in thy room. And it shall come to pass, that him that escapeth the sword of Hazael shall Jehu slay: and him that escapeth from the sword of Jehu shall Elisha slay. *Yet I have left me seven thousand in Israel, all the knees which have not bowed unto Baal, and every mouth which hath not kissed him* (1 Kings 19:5-18, KJV, emphasis added).

Can You Identify?

I hope you took time to read the previous passage. Though the passage is long, I specifically used the King James Version because of its wording. The italicized words reinforce Elijah's pride in himself and God's response to his pride.

If you did take some time to study it, we have a new jumping off point. From this summit, we can all have hope. Elijah fled and didn't have any direction from God concerning his dilemma; yet, God re-directed him. I'm sure when Elijah took off in the seemingly wrong direction that his adrenaline was on overload. Fear can do that. In fact, we can all function quite well on our own on adrenaline. But, adrenaline is not the fuel of the Holy Spirit. Adrenaline fuels the works of the flesh; the anointing is the fuel of the Spirit. Elijah ran away on his own adrenaline that was fueled by fear. We all know how to operate in our own fuel, don't we? Yes, we eventually hit the wall—a barrier—and experience some type of blockade, right?

Elijah ran, left his servant behind, and for forty days he was still running in his own strength—not empowered by God's directives. God didn't tell him to go there; he just went-because of fear! But, it is while he was in a cave, an isolated place, that he finally heard God's voice again. It had to have felt like another one of those long times. Let's analyze the entire passage that documents Elijah's wilderness journey, his attitude, and God's directives for the remainder of his life: Elijah thought he alone had to fulfill the purposes of God. How many times do we take on the burden of the Lord? Let's face it; we are not the Savior of the world! In fact if we feel that way, there is no way to win; failure is the result. I love how God addressed Elijah's attitude concerning his "I alone am left" attitude. God waited until Elijah was alone in a cave with failing adrenal glands for him to truly identify His voice. Elijah heard three sounds: a wind, an earthquake, and a still small voice. He didn't know it at the time, but Elijah was being trained at a whole new level to hear God's voice. We don't know exactly how he heard God's voice before this. But, we are about to understand how God gives grace to our pride, and then empowers us to fulfill our future. This is because He loves us, believes in us, and positions us to hear Him.

God Will Repeat Himself and Then Decide Not To!

It's true. God repeats Himself. Let's take wind for example. The first mention of it is in Genesis 8:1, in Noah's day, when God "sent a wind over the earth." Then, later on, Moses demonstrated God's power when he stretched out his staff over Egypt and the Lord made an "east wind blow." This wind caused locusts to completely devastate Egypt. But, the most memorable use of wind is when God sent another east wind and parted the waters of the Red Sea (see Exodus 14:22). This wind preserved and delivered the entire nation of God's people. Elijah, himself, had an experience with wind when he prayed, and the sky grew black with clouds and the "wind rose" (1 Kings 18:45).

Therefore, Elijah had surely heard about the "wind of God." In those days, stories were passed down concerning how God moved—so it would take much more than this to get

Elijah's attention. Understanding this, the wind alone did not make him come out of his cave. So, how about the earthquake? Well, again, there was great precedent concerning this. At Mount Sinai, the mountain shook (see Exodus 19:18). This sounds like an earthquake to me, doesn't it to you? That was in Moses' day. Let's move forward to Samuel's day when Jonathan had a vision to attack the Philistines and "the ground shook." It was seen as a panic sent by God. It is my thought that Elijah was still on a learning curve—though he thought he knew it all; there was now a hunger to hear His voice however He chose to deliver it! It was all about discerning the true presence of God. We all feel like failures when we think we heard His voice, but we miss it. Don't we? Believe me, I've been there. No fun.

So then there was fire. Surely that would cause him to come out of the cave, right? Fire was also part of God's calling card—so there's nothing new there. Elijah, himself called it down from heaven!

But, the still small voice was new. What was that? Elijah had never heard it before. Have I? Have you? I'm trying to train myself to hear it. It came at first when I ran. Yes, I ran from rejection, fear of abandonment, and fear of failure. It took a while, but over time I've learned how to position myself to hear it. But, Elijah is our example and I am thankful for it! He was learning to discern the true presence of the Lord. This is exactly where we also need to be positioned!

The Gentle Whisper That Empowers

After the fire of God, the gentle whisper of the Lord came to him (see again 1 Kings 19:12). It's a still, small voice. How do we recognize it? When do we hear it? I heard it when my mother was undergoing open-heart surgery. I was praying...a lot...and God interjected in my prayer and said, "I am going to heal your mother." I was stunned when I heard it—not expecting an interjection—as if He is on my timetable! But, when He said it, I knew it was God! It was the most profound experience. Nothing like it compares. It has happened several times since then, and I have learned to recognize it. I love it. Do I wait always on it before moving forward? No. But when I am in a test, when I feel like a failure and am depleted of self, He always finds me and softly calls me out of darkness!

God spoke to Elijah about his future in that place. He can speak to you about yours. Though you may see your life as a failure, God is still with you. Though you may be running away from God, He is faithful to find you and speak to you about fulfilling your destiny.

Elijah had a destiny to fulfill. So do you! He is speaking to you now. Can you discern His voice? You can go to a "fireball meeting" and experience a great move of God. When you prayed for the sick you may have felt His presence and His healing power. But what about those times when the enemy targets your identity? What about the time when you pray and someone is not healed? Do you run away, or do you press in? Elijah ran...we run...but the ultimate plan of God is *to always find us wherever we are.*

You Don't Have to Run

Dear one, you don't have to run away today...you can run *to*...God! As we discussed in the first chapter of this book, God loves you. Nothing can separate you from His love. If you believe you have messed up, run to Him. He awaits you; His arms are outstretched to you. His mercy endures forever. He has mercy just for you. Do you hear His still small voice speaking directly to you? He is calling your name right now. Press in. Hear Him calling your name. He knows you. He formed you before you were in your mother's womb. Don't' run away...run to God. Take time...now... and run...talk...express your fears, pain, and failures. Again, He looks forward to your running to Him; He will prove Himself faithful. He will greet you with open arms, love you, and empower you...just as He did Elijah...and give you hope for your future.

There is a plan for your life that was established before time. God has not forgotten it. We forget during times of stress, dissatisfaction, and discontentment. Take time right now and seek Him. He is not hard to find. He is readily available as close as your next breath! Your future awaits you as you ask, seek, and find.

A Time of Reflection

I have heard someone once say that *grace* is God giving us heaven's best at Christ's expense. I love that definition of grace and fully believe it is true. I have also studied grace and found it to represent God's unmerited favor. Still there is another definition of grace to which I relate—and I believe maybe even Elijah (a man like us) could relate: grace is the divine empowerment from God to fulfill His calling upon our lives while demonstrating His Kingdom on earth.

1.   Which definition of grace do you relate to the most and why?

2.   Since Elijah was a man like us, how would you describe Elijah's being empowered with God's grace?

3.   Considering "pride" and "self," have you encountered seasons when the Holy Spirit is ministering to you about your relationship to Him and your attitude concerning yourself? If so, describe below.

4.   Have you experienced failure and then realized too much of "you" was involved in the situation? Faith in your results in less faith in God. It's difficult to have faith once more when great loss has occurred; however, it is possible! Be like Elijah today and position yourself to hear the voice of God. Elijah had to completely run out of steam to hear properly. Maybe you've come to the end of yourself and for the first time feel that you are really ready to hear Him. Take a few moments to hear. Write below what the Lord is saying to your heart.

CHAPTER 5

When the Disciples Failed

It was not just an ordinary day for the disciples. It was a homecoming! Anxious to share their testimonies, they kept interrupting each other. There was enormous energy generated in their midst...so much so that crowds began to gather out of curiosity.

Just days before, Jesus had sent them out by two's and had given them power over the unclean spirits. And now, meeting in Capernaum, their hearts were filled with enthusiasm and excitement as they shared the power of God demonstrated among the people. They could barely wait to see the Teacher and share the miracles each had witnessed. These disciples of Jesus had cast out demons, anointed the sick with oil, and witnessed healings. They were bursting with joy as each testified what had occurred on their journeys.

"There He is!" said one of the disciples as he spotted Jesus and pointed toward His direction. The entire group began running full speed toward Him, and before coming to a complete stop, they were each attempting to tell his story first. Understanding their enthusiasm, Jesus signaled with a smile that silently spoke... it's okay...calm down, you'll get your chance to testify of all that you saw the Father do.

Jesus took his time with each disciple as He embraced each of them separately. Such overwhelming love flowed from Him; it was almost incomprehensible. He had a unique way that made each disciple feel special. It was like a family gathering—coming back together to share all they had seen. After all, there was much to rejoice about since Jesus had given them power over the spirits of darkness. Their faith reached watermark levels as they had wrought miracles and taught others by using the name of Jesus.

More crowds were gathering and soon there was a multitude of people surrounding Jesus and His disciples. There was so much activity they hadn't even had a chance to eat so Jesus said to them, "Come with me by yourselves to a quiet place and get some rest" (Mark 6:31b).

Peter looked to John and sighed in relief knowing that if he was exhausted and hungry, John and the others must be also. They made their way to a boat and headed to a solitary place. Peter and John grabbed an oar and the other disciples filed into place and helped. "Finally," Peter thought to himself, "we can get some quality rest and something to eat." But, the crowd recognized them and ran to get ahead of them. When Jesus and the disciples reached their destination across the water, a throng of people awaited them. Jesus gazed at the multitude that sought Him and *immediately* had great compassion because they were like sheep without a shepherd. So, instead of resting, Jesus began teaching the crowd many things concerning the kingdom of God.

Peter, John, James, and the other disciples noticed the crowd also. Then, after mentally attempting to calculate how long Jesus might need to minister to these people, they became completely overwhelmed. In fact, they looked at each other in despair. No words needed to be exchanged between them. Inwardly, they were screaming, "It's getting late; I'm hungry and I'm even more exhausted!" Their minds and emotions were out of control. They knew that when they saw Jesus' eyes of compassion light upon a need—their individual needs went *immediately* to the back burner—or at least that was their perception. However, Jesus knew that everything He did was done because Heaven had destined it, and He was always quite confident that the disciples would learn and adjust. After all, He was not bent on pleasing men, but completely devoted to pleasing the Father.

After a few minutes of frustration, the disciples gravitated to a common consensus; they needed to remind Jesus, somehow, that they had just returned from a long mission trip, and they needed rest and food. The disciples decided the best way to get Jesus to see their needs was for them to act more concerned for the "people" by reminding Jesus that they were in a remote place, and it was late. They would deliberately point out to Him that the "others" were probably hungry and needed to leave. They elected Peter to do the talking for them as he was always the most zealous.

Standing before Jesus, Peter piped up and said, "Jesus, I'm concerned that these people are probably hungry. After all, it's very late. Don't you think You need to send them back to the village so they can buy something to eat?" All the disciples shook their heads in agreement with Peter, not really considering the needs of the crowd, but focusing on their own need to rest and eat!

Instead of heeding their advice, Jesus looked at the disciples and said something so alarming to them, "*You* give them something to eat" (Mark 6:37, emphasis added). I know, talk about pressure! Jesus told them to feed the multitudes!

SUPERNATURAL PROVISION = GIVE WHAT YOU HAVE & EXPECT GOD TO MULTIPLY IT.

Peter looked at John with a "What did He say?" look. John was searching for any extra change he might have. The other disciples stood completely stunned. They all knew that to feed that many people it would take eight months of wages! "Jesus," they exclaimed, "Do you want us to go and spend all of our money on bread for them? We don't have enough for that!"

Jesus was still in His teaching mode. He was preparing Himself to teach His disciples another lesson. This time it would be a lesson of supernatural provision: give what you have and expect God to multiply it. So Jesus said to His disciples, "How many loaves do you have?...Go and see" (Mark 6:38a).

The disciples went and examined how much food they had, returned and told Jesus that they had only five loaves left and two fish. Knowing that was not nearly enough food to feed that large crowd, they prepared themselves to return to the boat; but, Jesus had a miracle in mind. Instead of releasing the people, He directed the disciples to divide the people into groups and have them sit down on the green grass.

The minds of the disciples ran wild again! "What in the world?" Peter thought. James stood still, but was shaking his head in disbelief, muttering to himself, "Surely Jesus knows how tired we are and how hungry 'they' are!" However, they did as instructed and had the crowds sit in groups of hundreds and fifties.

After the people were quieted and seated, Jesus took the five loaves and the two fish. He looked up to heaven and gave thanks for the provision they had received from the Father and then He broke the loaves. He next divided the two fish among the disciples to set before the people. The disciples each looked at what they were to feed the multitudes: a partial loaf of bread and two divided fish.

The disciples looked at the sliver of fish and the partial loaves and then looked at each other. Again, their minds were on tilt! Yet, they went forth as instructed with what little they had to feed the multitude. To their amazement each time a piece of bread and fish was given, they would look in their baskets and there was even more bread and fish added. Each time they passed a portion to someone in the crowd they witnessed multiplication!

The disciples, themselves, were part of this miracle! "They" were giving this crowd something to eat. Out of their faith in what Jesus instructed them to do, a miracle occurred. There was enough food for the crowd to have seconds! All together the disciples fed 5,000 men and that didn't include women and children. Now, this was certainly a miracle testimony to take with them on the next mission trip!

Immediately after this miracle, Jesus made his disciples get back into the boat and go ahead of Him to Bethsaida. Jesus dismissed the crowd and then went up to a mountainside to spend time in prayer.

Nightfall came. Jesus was alone on land, but His disciples were in the boat in the middle of the lake and without Jesus! A large storm appeared and the disciples were straining at the oars of the boat, fearing for their lives. Jesus saw their struggle and walked out to them on the water.

But rather than have faith, the disciples feared for their lives. As part of their test, Jesus deliberately appeared to pass them by, checking the level of their faith, He waited for their responses. Unfortunately, they didn't even imagine it might be Jesus and instead thought He was a ghost. After all, who can walk on water? There was now a new lesson for the disciples to learn. Another curve ball headed their way; hopefully, they would swing correctly for a home run! But no, they didn't even make it to first base.

The disciples cried out in fear. Mark 6:50 says that He spoke to them and said, "Take courage! It is I. Don't be afraid." Then Jesus climbed into the boat with His disciples. As soon as Jesus did this, the wind died down and the disciples were amazed.

There Is More to This Story

Precious reader, I chose to end this story before I get to the punch line on purpose. First, thank you again for allowing me to use my imagination a bit to paint another picture of biblical history. I love to think about the disciples' expressions, their inner thoughts and, yes, maybe their uncircumcised motives! It makes me feel that I can fit in their category somewhat—a disciple who is still in training. Maybe you can also relate.

Still, I want you to notice the word "immediately" in this story. It is mentioned twice in this account from the NIV version, and I italicized it in this text purposefully. When the

WE NEED IMMEDIATE FAITH FOR IMMEDIATE RESULTS,

same word is mentioned more than once in the same chapter or verse, there is an intention involved. It is a word only used a few times in the Old Testament, but noticed a multitude of times in the New Testament. Jesus got "immediate" results. When He prayed for the woman with the issue of blood she was *immediately* healed. (Luke 8:47, NLT). Matthew 21:19 reminds us that when Jesus cursed a fig tree it immediately withered up and died. Luke 4:39 shares the testimony of how Jesus prayed for Simon's mother who had a fever. When He prayed for her she *immediately* rose up healed. The list goes on and on. I encourage you to do a study on how many *immediately's* there are in the New Testament.

The word "immediately" in Greek is *parachrema* and means "instantly or straightway." We were "immediately" given *sozo* when we became Christians. We talked about this earlier, but *sozo* is "everything heaven has to offer us." We need to lock into that word, *immediately*. If we are sick and we ask for prayer, we must put our faith in His Word that states, "By His stripes we *were* healed." Notice the past tense here? This means it has already been purchased by Jesus at the cross! Hallelujah! Yes, we need *immediate* faith for *immediate* results! Yet we know that our faith is not in our abilities, but rather faith in Jesus, and His finished work.

Wait! There's more to this word *parachrema*— immediately. Notice the second half of this word is *chrema* which bumps up the full understanding of this word meaning "immediately." *Chrema* is connected to something that is "needed," (by someone or for someone), something useful, but it is also connected to "wealth" and "price." You might be wondering just why I consider this important. Jesus wants to give us exactly what is needed. Whether it be healing, provision, or deliverance—whatever is needed—He desires to use what He established at the cross to provide it for you. And, dear one, did you notice that the words "wealth" and "price" are also connected to this study? Jesus paid a price to give you whatever you need. There is a wealth of promises in the Word that are available to each of us. Remember, He is faithful! What He promises—He will do for you!

Why am I hammering in the faithfulness of God again? Well, as you will read later, our salvation is strongly connected to the faithfulness of God. Because He is faithful, He provided salvation from the beginning of the foundation of the world. Also, when we experience His faithfulness, it increases our faith in God. The disciples feared the storm because they did not understand God's faithfulness. After the feeding of the five thousand it should have proven God's love to them and His desire to care for their every need. In fact, the Scripture says that they had "hard hearts!" Ouch. Let's be real about God's nature. Can you take some time and go there with me just a bit? We all need to understand that a hard heart is not pleasing to God. In fact, it is every bit connected to legalism, Pharisaism, doubt, and unbelief. Hebrews 11:6 states, "Without faith it is impossible to please God." Therefore, I feel that it is safe to consider unbelief a form of sin. Unbelief manifests as doubting God and His promises. It nullifies the finished work of Christ by exalting the "works" of the flesh.

When the Disciples Failed

To think on the fact that Jesus' disciples may have fallen short at times is difficult for me. I grew up in a church that pictured them on stained glass windows—all the way from the front left wall to the back right wall! I'd sit in the pew on Sunday mornings and ponder the images of their faces, length of their hair, their beards—or no beard—and the color of their clothing. It was easy to conclude which was Jesus as He always had a staff and sheep around him. But, the disciples were more challenging to discern.

Observing the glass characters was much more inviting to a five year old than the pastor's sermon. I idolized those whom Jesus discipled for being chosen to walk with Him on a daily basis and for the hands—on mentoring they received. Since this book is on faith after failure, I might as well mention the one disciple who most obviously missed the mark—Judas, of course. And, then there was Peter, who was one of my favorite character studies as a child because after all, he walked on water! Wow! Somehow I missed the fact that his faith failed him and he sank. Oh, and I believe I actually cried when my Sunday school teacher said that Jesus addressed him as satan when He said to Peter, "Get thee behind me, satan." Yet, over the years I have admired Peter—even through his human weaknesses. More on Peter in chapter nine.

The disciples were fearful in the storm. (Most of us are tempted in the same way!) This could be considered a failure of some sort—couldn't it? After all, the Word states that without faith it is impossible to please God. Our faith is in His ability to perform His Word—such as providing divine protection; especially in a storm. Yet, though their faith failed them when the waves crashed against the boat, Jesus was right on time with an impartation of courage and faith! Think about it. They had just been part of a miracle: "they" fed the crowd. Then, Jesus sent them to the other side. Yet, when encountering a storm they forgot that Jesus sent them forth fully expecting them to get there! After all, what Jesus said would happen always happened. Yet, still, they doubted

Guarding our Hearts

Let's re-visit the event of the disciples rowing hard against the strong winds after the feeding of the people. It is clear—they were absolutely horrified. Again, we might ask ourselves how that could possibly happen after they witnessed such an incredible miracle. Yet, they were human, just like you and me. Let's put ourselves in their place for a moment. Can you imagine what they might be thinking? Like...*where's Jesus? Great, He sends us in a boat to the other side. He leaves us to go off and pray. We get into the storm and He's safe on shore. Seems like something is wrong with this picture!* Maybe they thought: J*esus cares more about those **other people** more than us. **We're** the ones who are the disciples. We forsook all to follow Him and yet He cares more about **them** receiving food and rest than He does us!*

Maybe you can relate. When our lives are challenged with trauma, unbelief creeps in. We wonder: *"Where's God? Doesn't He know I am hurting?"*

However, we must be careful to always guard our hearts. In Mark 6:52, the Amplified Version gives us a key as we attempt to understand just why the disciples developed hard hearts. Let's take a look and please notice the italicized words for more introspection:

> For they *failed* to consider or understand [the teaching and meaning of the miracle of] the loaves; [in fact] their hearts had grown callous [had become

dull and had lost the power of understanding]
(Mark 6:52, AMP).

Did you get it? The disciples *failed.* Now we are in good company if we have also failed. Let's just go ahead and admit it—we have failed also! It's okay to admit it! Other than fear, how else did they fail? Well, precious believer, the Word shares that they did not "consider" or understand the miracle of the loaves! Oh, my. How soon we forget God's faithfulness. We get a breakthrough, and then a storm comes and we immediately forget the previous breakthrough we just experienced. The disciples themselves fed the people and they had already forgotten the power they had. Before Jesus intervened, there was enough anointing in that boat to rebuke the storm; yet fear crowded out faith.

Dear one, please do not receive this example with condemnation. I have written on this passage so that we might recognize the fact that we all have a measure of faith. And, yet, there are times that the Holy Spirit reminds us that the "righteousness of God is revealed from faith to faith; as it is written, 'The just shall live by faith'" (Romans 1:17, NKJV).

This passage reminds us that it is the "righteousness" of God that is revealed to us as we develop progressive faith. Understanding this further, we realize that it is not our own righteousness that empowers us with greater faith—it is faith in His righteousness that releases grace and a supernatural empowerment to become more like Him and move in more of the supernatural power of God! We are continually being transformed into His divine image and, therefore, becoming more like Him. However, we do not do the transforming; it is His DNA within our spirits that brings forth changes that are needed to develop stronger faith. For now, focus on the righteousness of Christ. As you do, your faith will develop to a new level.

Failing to Consider

Back to the miracle when a storm arose that the disciples failed to consider. Let's be honest and ask ourselves: have we also, at times, failed to "consider?" Let me be blunt again *only* for the sake of getting straight to your heart. If we don't "consider" what God has done, we have failed in our attempt to abandon ourselves in Him and trusting in His ability to do abundantly more than we could ever ask or think! Now, again, don't hit the fast forward button and eventually default in guilt and shame. Give me a moment to explain. The word "consider" means that we give "attention" to something. What we give attention to becomes high priority in our lives. Take a moment and examine your thought life. Do you give more attention to the negative? Do you focus on lack or loss? Do you spotlight "failure" rather than shift into greater faith which is available to you? And, precious believer, are we more focused on ourselves and our abilities rather than what Christ desires to do through us? In other words, are we being led by the Spirit or the flesh? We will talk more about this in great length later, but for now know that our life is not our own. Let me explain. Christ died for us so that we could live in Him (see 2 Corinthians 5:15).

One day I actually had a vision of this. I was worshiping in church and suddenly I was caught away in a vision. I saw myself placed in the heart of Jesus Christ on the cross at Calvary. When Christ died and said, "It is finished," I saw myself die. But, I also saw myself resurrected with Him into life! It then became Christ living in me. I was still dead, but yet alive only because He lived in me!

If we "fail to consider" this miraculous truth, we err in the same way as did the disciples. We have resurrection power within us, and the disciples had the directives of Jesus daily encouraging them. Therefore, as a believer I can now fully believe that I can do all things through Christ who strengthens me! And, also that nothing is impossible to me because I believe!

The word "consider" is laced all through the Old and New Testaments. One of my favorite passages is Psalm 77:12 says, "I will meditate also upon all Your works and consider all Your [mighty] deeds" (AMP). When I am troubled and I am experiencing any form of demonic opposition, I quote Psalm 119:95 which states that I "consider" His testimonies of faithfulness, "The wicked wait for me to destroy me, but I will consider Your testimonies" (AMP).

But, my all time favorite passage is when Jesus is speaking about not being anxious and that worry avails us nothing. Study carefully the passage below. Look at what Jesus says about our need to "consider:"

> And who of you by worrying and being anxious can add one unit of measure (cubit) to his stature or to the span of his life? And why should you be anxious about clothes? Consider the lilies of the field and learn thoroughly how they grow; they neither toil nor spin. Yet I tell you, even Solomon in all his magnificence (excellence, dignity, and grace) was not arrayed like one of these. But if God

99

so clothes the grass of the field, which today is alive and green and tomorrow is tossed into the furnace, will He not much more surely clothe you, O you of little faith? Therefore do not worry and be anxious, saying, What are we going to have to eat? or, What are we going to have to drink? or, What are we going to have to wear? For the Gentiles (heathen) wish for and crave and diligently seek all these things, and your heavenly Father knows well that you need them all. But seek (aim at and strive after) first of all His kingdom and His righteousness (His way of doing and being right), and then all these things taken together will be given you besides. So do not worry or be anxious about tomorrow, for tomorrow will have worries and anxieties of its own. Sufficient for each day is its own trouble (Matthew 6:27-34, AMP).

Precious saint of God, do you realize that what you consider (think on, ponder) you eventually become. The Word says, "For as he thinketh in his heart, so is he" (Proverbs 23:7a, KJV). I believe it is safe to say that Proverbs 23:7 is also saying to us that what you consider in your heart will determine if your heart becomes hard or not. Refer back to when the disciples did not "consider" the feeding of the multitudes and their hearts were hardened.

Jesus talked about hard hearts quite often. Let's do a quick study on this because it will lay a platform on which we can launch into greater faith. Remember, the disciples failed to recognize and consider all that had previously happened: how Jesus miraculously provided and how they were a part of the miracle! However, they were able later to continue as Jesus' disciples and remained positioned to shift into great faith. How were they able to do this? Well, one thing for sure, their hearts had to change. A thought for us to consider at this point is that maybe our hearts needs to change also. If we are not witnessing promised breakthroughs and divine encounters of power and demonstration, could the problem be us? Could the problem be a hard heart? Well, let's examine this more closely. Keep reading; victory awaits your arrival!

Hard Hearts Lead to Destruction and Failure

The ultimate hard-hearted one (and he was an angel!) was Lucifer. Isaiah 14:13 describes how Lucifer said "in his heart" that he would ascend above God. Again, as I mentioned earlier, since the time that the devil was removed by God from his self-exalted position, he has targeted those that God loves, both saved and unsaved. He attempts to blind God's people to truth and builds a case against God in our minds and hearts which results in hard-heartedness and rebellion. Still, we must consider the fact that many times we, as believers, are influenced by satan and his evil seductions. If at any time we attempt to believe we have a better way, a better plan, or another road other than God's direction, we have also "said in our hearts" that we will ascend above God and His plans for our lives. I have written an entire book concerning how satan lies to us, robbing us of our faith, and ultimately our destiny. I would encourage you to read *Silencing the Accuser: Eight Lies Satan Uses Against Christians* (Chosen Books, 2011) if you struggle with your identity in Christ or continual doubt and unbelief.

Pharaoh is another prime example of someone with a hard heart. God even used his hard-heartedness to ultimately

101

loose the Israelites. If you recall, it was the last plague which took the life of the firstborn that caused Pharaoh to let God's people go from Egyptian bondage. God instructed Moses to have each Israelite family slay a lamb and smear its blood upon the lintels (beams) and doorposts of every house. This action protected the first born from the death angel. How, you ask? Well, many have erroneously taught that the blood on the doorposts of the homes told the death angel to allow that household to escape. But, actually the blood on the doorpost said to the death angel that there had already been a death extracted there. The death of the lamb signified the death of the firstborn since Jesus is the Lamb of God, the firstborn of the Father. This substitutionary death is still represented at the feast of Passover today.

All of this was a shadow of what was to come. The Blood of Jesus is the ultimate sacrifice and continues to break the power of death over us. Simply reminding ourselves of this fact will keep our hearts softened before the Lord. Remembering the price Jesus paid for our freedom still tenders my heart. I'm sure if you continue to "consider" what Jesus did, it will do the same for you! Sometimes we must continue to remind ourselves of the fact that we were bought with a great price: the blood of Jesus. Keeping this in mind will keep an important concept at the forefront of our belief system; we are joint-heirs in Christ Jesus, and we have a royal inheritance! Reminding ourselves of this will plow our hearts and prepare the soil for more of His life-changing Word.

Hebrews chapter three verses eight and fifteen warns us to not harden our hearts toward God as the children of Israel did in the wilderness. If you recall, the entire time the Israelites were in the wilderness they murmured, complained, and basically rebelled against God. Even when God performed miracles, they went right back into an ungodly cycle. Sad that they didn't "consider" the miracles they witnessed. Their unbelief ultimately blocked their entrance into the Promised Land. Please keep in mind that it did not mean they did not go to heaven and neither does it mean that unbelief keeps us from an eternity with God. It does mean, however, that unbelief will rob us of breakthroughs that are needed here on earth and that it negates faith to receive the promises of God.

> **HAVING A HARD HEART WILL KEEP US WANDERING IN THE WILDERNESS.**

Avoiding a Hard Heart

Having a hard heart will keep us wandering in the wilderness and not witnessing God's best. This entire book is being written for the purpose of empowering you with faith and godly success, and a hard heart can steal those very areas from you! You are probably asking what I have also asked, "What will protect my heart from becoming hard?" I'm glad you asked that question. Let me explain the way you can protect your heart:

1. **Fix your mind and heart completely on God rather than the things of this world.** Colossians 3:2 says, "Set your mind on things above, not on things on the earth" (NKJV). This means basically that our affections should be bent toward heaven and Kingdom purposes. We need a wake-up call periodically concerning eternity, wouldn't you agree? Our purpose on earth is to show forth His glory—not our own,

right? Being overly concerned for our own lives and having our affections centered on things that hinder our walk with Christ will empower the heart to *close* the door to *God's* plans concerning our lives.

2. **Exercise a repentant heart.** We need to always be listening to the leading of the Holy Spirit. If He speaks to us concerning a need to repent (change our minds), we should do so quickly! Repentance does not mean that we are expecting God to punish us for doing something wrong. No way! Jesus took all guilt and shame to the cross as He died for our sins. Our sins are forgiven—yesterday, today and forever! Still, when we sin, the Holy Spirit will speak to us concerning our identity. When we sin, we are not acting like God's redeemed child, are we? A repentant heart will always recognize God's desire to forgive, but at the same time be willing to receive grace to change and be restored.

3. **Position yourself for obedience.** When I mention the word "obedience," do you cringe? I hope not! I used to do that, c-r-i-n-g-e, when I heard that word. I could almost picture this cowering dog that has been harshly trained and disciplined to submit to the master's commands! But, that is not God's way at all. He loves us, yes, and disciplines us, but never with the intention to hurt us, strike us, or withhold from us! *Remember, Jesus was struck once and for all on the cross.* He paid the price for our sin and

works of the flesh. As I have understood more concerning God's divine grace, I now know that to be obedient to God's directives requires me to receive His grace to fulfill what He asks of me. I can only fulfill what He desires by receiving His grace or else I will get into works. Works are fulfilling God's desires through self-strength and self-determination. There is no room for both grace and self in the heart of a believer. This is because Christ is grace; He alone consumes our hearts!

Let's Hear the Voice of Jesus Today

It is time, today, to hear the voice of Jesus! Take this admonition also as a solemn warning: **take time *today* while there is still a *today* to hear Him**. I have heard it said that a procrastinator will not take "now" for an answer! Yet, He is asking for your attention now. Will you hear? Let's look at Hebrews 3:7-9, which is the New Testament exhortation to hear His voice today:

> Therefore, as the Holy Spirit says: Today, if you will hear His voice, Do not harden your hearts, as [happened] in the rebellion [of Israel] and their provocation and embitterment [of Me] in the day of testing in the wilderness, Where your fathers tried [My patience] and tested [My forbearance] and found I stood their test, and they saw My works for forty years (AMP).

Think for a moment. *Today,* if you will hear His voice, harden not your hearts. If we take this admonition seriously, we realize that He asks for your attention, your heart, your soul, your all; but He uses no compulsion. If you will hear! You are being ministered to by the Holy Spirit right now, at this very moment, to hear Him and not harden your heart concerning giving your all to Him!

A careful study of Psalm 95:7 also encourages us to seek God today. It explains that we are the sheep of His "pasture" and the sheep of His "hand" (KJV). We are encouraged not to harden our hearts as Israel did at Meribah and Massah which were places that represented bitterness and bitter waters. If you recall, the children of Israel murmured the entire time they wandered in the wilderness. They were bitter toward God, and they hardened their hearts. Let me be blunt: bitterness, unthankfulness, murmuring, and complaining birth hard hearts toward God. These attitudes will almost guarantee failure because we won't seek Him; we won't run to the throne and fellowship with Him and receive grace for our future!

Let's close this chapter with a heart search. Is there bitterness, unthankfulness, or resentment toward God which is infecting your heart and attitude toward Him? If so, do not be afraid to run to Him, NOW! Shame will send you on a wilderness hike, but when you realize that there is nothing that can separate you from His love, not even murmuring and complaining. Let's be real and call it "having a really yucky attitude!" Remember, that today is a day to seek Him and not run away from His presence. Think about this: what if the disciples had become bitter because they felt like failures and then abandoned their Master? I know that when He was crucified they scattered a bit, but their hearts led them home to Him. But what about you? Have you been disappointed, shamed, or felt as a failure? I have. Bet you have, too. It's time for a heart check. Take a few moments for Self Reflection and then move on to the next chapter. I will meet you there!

A Time of Reflection

1. Do you recall a time in your life where you were disappointed? Is that disappointment still there? Can you identify how it might be affecting you today? Maybe you have withdrawn from God, ashamed of something connected to your past. Could it be that you feel like a complete failure right now, and you have hardened your heart, refusing to hear His voice concerning your situation? Write below any disappointment, fear, shame...anything that blocks you from receiving His love and divine grace:

2. Now, see yourself approaching God's throne. His arms are open wide to receive you. He desires to heal your pain and to also mend your heart. Jesus Christ shed His precious blood to completely set you free from any failure, guilt, or memory of the past that continues to haunt you. Go ahead, talk to Him...now. Don't delay any longer; He desires to talk to you.

3.   Lastly, take a few moments and write a prayer below. Include areas you need mended, healed and restored. As you document your feelings, take a few extra moments and thank the Lord for Jesus and His obedience to go to the cross on your behalf. Write down any other thoughts that the Holy Spirit brings to your heart. You are not limited to document my suggestions; the Holy Spirit is your teacher and He will guide you as you seek Him and write.

4.   Now, I would like for you to picture the cross, with all of your shame, fear, loss, failure (etc) nailed to it with Jesus. Boldly declare, "My sins were nailed to the cross with Jesus. My failure, shame, disappointment, (name whatever else the Holy Spirit brings to your mind) were also nailed to the cross. Because of what Jesus accomplished at the cross, shedding His blood as the ultimate sacrifice, I am free!" Then, finally see yourself on the other side of the cross completely covered with the shed blood of Jesus. Yes! This is your today of victory!

CHAPTER 6

The Failure to Measure Up

"A bend in the road is not the end of the road...
unless you fail to make the turn."
~Anonymous

A yardstick can be an incredible tool if it is used with the right intention. It's an instrument with which one takes measurements. My dad had one when I was a child that he kept in his office closet. We lived in a very small house in Lubbock, Texas at the time, and I still remember that closet because it contained an escape hatch underneath the floor for tornadoes. For me, that closet has been forever connected to dad's measuring stick! And, precious believers, I still remember it to this day. In fact, that is perhaps why I teach: measuring = escaping. Think about it. Maybe you can identify with the measuring = escaping ideology. Most of us run in the opposite direction or escape if we believe that we are being challenged to measure up to a specific standard. Sure, we want to believe we enjoy a challenge, but so often there is an underlying sense of dread along with a voice-blast-from-our-past, saying, "What happens if you fail?" The bottom line is that no one ever wants to fall short of hitting the mark.

Dad's measuring stick was an odd color of orange! Maybe it was a pre-mature glow in the dark stick, and we didn't know it. All I could tell as a child was that it was ugly! It's possible that he picked that color because it was easy to locate in the dimly lit closet. But, knowing dad, it was probably on sale and regardless of how ridiculously offensive the color, he needed it. Bargain prices—I have learned to shop like him. Even today, there is a gravity pull in the direction of a sale. Maybe discounted items scream out to me the loudest: buy me—whether you need me or not! Buy ME! My home closets are packed with items I really didn't need, but they were such a great price! Stay with me...I'm going somewhere. I promise that this chapter will offer opportunities to shift out of a lifestyle which sets you up for continual failure. Let your faith arise even more as you continue to read.

The Sense of Lack

A few years ago, my husband and I relocated to a beautiful new ranch in North Fort Worth, Texas. It's a lovely home with a large barn, lots of trees, and room for horses. While unpacking I once again realized that I have way too much stuff! Much of the stuff was bought on sale thinking I just might need it someday. Maybe you can relate. Well, while I was unpacking I realized that it was ten years ago that I purchased a screaming out loud "BUY ME" object, and I still hadn't used it! It was time to let go. Time to toss the extra garbage (oops! I should say baggage, right?). I tossed out so much stuff and began to calculate approximately how much I saved my husband by buying what was on sale. I'm embarrassed to say how much I spent on those items that I never used. Some of the price tags were still on the clothing I had purchased.

Allow me to be vulnerable for a moment. I unpacked designer rain galoshes that I had purchased...just in case. I also unpacked a zebra-striped umbrella that would match my zebra-striped sweater, but who would remember to wear both together on a rainy day? Even yet, I'd have to wait for it to actually rain to get the full benefit of the matching set!

Oh, and then there was the hat. No, it wasn't a rain hat, it was an Easter hat. Needless to say that it was an adorable Easter bonnet hat in every way-flower, ribbon, the whole nine yards! The problem was that it was large...very large. So large it blocked the view of the person behind me in church. One person came up to me after the service with neck pain; he insinuated that his neck was out of joint trying to see the minister. He said that he came to church that morning fine, but left needing to visit his chiropractor!

And then, there was the pasta machine I purchased, and I hardly ever eat pasta! Much less go to the trouble to make it! Oh, I had high hopes of someday being Suzy Homemaker, but the Suzy in me never showed up and neither did Betty Crocker.

I know you've seen movies about the day-after-Thanksgiving sales; well, let me confess to you that I almost lost my salvation when a lady grabbed the only black dress in my size right out of my hands! My knee-jerk response was to yank it back, but I let the woman have it. I'm honest when I say I think that I was so mad that my eyeballs almost popped out of my head; I couldn't believe it! No respect at all! But, then there was the time I almost did the same to someone else. Sale-shoppers are destined to also be risk-takers! Did you realize that? You are a risk-taker; it's commendable! Yes, after all the trouble of beating someone else to the sale rack there is a huge risk that someone might show up at the Christmas party with an exact match to your dress!

Now for you men readers who might be rolling your eyes right now while reading this testimony, please let me say this: maybe you don't chase blue-light specials, but you should have seen my pastor husband complaining that his 30% discount on golf gloves had expired!

Okay, back to unpacking my stuff at the ranch. After the twentieth box of donations to the Goodwill®, I sat down and began to cry. What have I done? I am not a compulsive spender; in fact, I can be quite frugal when I want to be. I know how to budget money, and I'm very good in working with my husband in the area of investments. But, I began a quick heart search for answers as to what was driving me to this type of behavior? I realized, once again I might add, that there was a compelling sense of lack in my life. Yes, like a vacuum that draws everything down a dark hole, there was an uncontrollable feeling of being "less than" and a debilitating sense of always feeling that I needed to "measure up."

As I continued to sob that one day, the Lord spoke very clearly to my heart. He reminded me of my dad's yardstick. I remembered him taking that yardstick out periodically and measuring my height. It was a way to measure growth. Since we all want to grow up to be "big," I looked forward to those measuring times, viewing the pencil marks on the walls and being proud that I had grown. However, as the Lord dealt with me all I could focus on was the fact that I was still attempting to "measure up" in life.

"Measuring Up" is Exhausting

Is it really worth the trouble? By that I mean, is it really worth the effort of beating everyone to the punch? Do we always have to be the one who "wins"? Or, be the one who is the most "recognized"? I believe you just might understand what I mean; we have all been compared to someone else in life by our parents, a teacher, or maybe a coach. We have all felt as if there were someone else that might take our place if we didn't compete and fight for it! Every one of us at some time in life has most likely had someone we desire to become like. My goal was to be another Debbie Reynolds (some of you reading may not identify, but believe me she is awesome even today as I write!) Some of you men who are reading this book may want to be another football icon such as Tom Landry, the former Dallas Cowboy Coach, or Tiger Woods who is one of the world's leading golfers ever.

Unfortunately, many preachers teach from the pulpit about standards of holiness and righteousness (and I was once one of them!), all the while connecting holiness to religious works! Holiness...righteousness...it's been taught for decades, but way too often with a wrong revelation. The truth is that Christ, alone, is righteous. We are only righteous in Him! If we are expected to be righteous on our own, we are in for an impossible task.

It can seem to some as if God has His own measuring stick hidden away in His closet somewhere waiting to pull it out and measure whether or not we have achieved a standard or goal, or if we are acceptable at that juncture in life! If we believe that about our Father, we waste years of our lives in despair. We will seek acceptance from all the wrong sources; we will do our "darndest" to be better than all the rest; we will push ourselves to be fit enough to run every race only to realize that it's never good enough when a void in our lives fuel our future.

Dear ones, we are only righteous due to the fact that we are born again. When we receive Jesus Christ as our personal Lord and Savior, we become a new man or woman in Christ. We then become righteous because He, alone, is righteous. The need to "measure up" comes from our past when we experienced failure. Our memory of failing is etched into our memory—like a computer chip. But that computer chip can be removed! How? Through the renewing of our minds!

Renewing the Mind

Renewing the mind is not as difficult as you might think. So many Christians think it is difficult, but it's really simple. I know that I have personally spent years asking God to renew my mind. I had no idea that it would be God Himself that would take charge in doing it! Yes, for many years, I thought it was up to me to renew my mind. To a degree, that is completely true. I do have to position myself as a daughter of God to receive instruction from my Father in Heaven. This is the first step in renewing our minds.

So many of us believe that He is going to invade our minds all at once, and we go to sleep one night and wake up with a renewed mind. This is a misconception of how God works in us. Though He can do that, it is has been my experience as local pastor and leader in the Body of Christ that He takes His time in renewing our minds! So please don't be discouraged if your mind has not shifted yet; He has eternity to renew our minds!

Once the pressure is off for us to be perfect we are positioned to have our minds renewed and free to talk with God again. This is because we do not feel ashamed because of our past, and we can run to his arms and talk to Him. When we feel His love, knowing we are fully 100% accepted, we can talk freely to Him and express our hearts, fears, and concerns. What we experience in the position as sons and daughters of God empowers us to shift from a place of feeling unworthy with a need to consistently measure up to a position of receiving all He has for us as sons and daughters. Know that you are a son or daughter of the Most High which will give you a place with your Father in heaven. You don't have to fight for prominence any longer! You have it now! Lock onto the fact that God loves you; you are His child!

Attempting to beat anyone else at anything is completely exhausting. Allow me to once again be blunt for a moment: this type of behavior is rooted in ungodly competition (ask me how I know!), a sense of lack, and unworthiness. Please understand that if there is any fear of not "measuring up" in life, we will forever be compelled to compete against others and remain in a performance mode—even performing to please God!

Trying to be righteous in our own strength is impossible. After all, which one of us can measure up to the righteousness of Christ? We can't do it, and God knows it!

Sons of God

"I will be a Father to you, and you will be my **sons and daughters**, says the Lord Almighty" (2 Corinthians 6:18).

God calls us "sons," and I will use the term "sons" to include both sons are daughters in God. So, when reading about "sons," the daughters can also relate! Sons are no longer servants when they receive Christ as their savior. A servant believes he is doomed to a form of imprisonment, like a type of slave. But a son knows his father, and also realizes that he can approach his loving father and speak to him at any time necessary.

With this in mind, I want you as a male or female to think about this question for a moment and ask yourself: is a beautiful dress, a make-over, or is a great golf score really a true measurement of who you are? Let me assure you that Sandie Freed, the author of the book you now hold in your hands, had to ask herself the same question: what is defining my identity?

While unpacking that day about which I previously wrote, I finally realized, once again, that I was still attempting to measure up to some type of idealistic way that I needed to look and present myself to others. I also realized that the cycle of lack—measuring up—and unworthiness is a continuous cycle. Dear ones, let me assure you that all three of these are connected. In this chapter, I am focused on defining how we are deceived into believing that we must "measure up" to someone else's standards other than God's. At the same time, our sense of lack and unworthiness fuels our need to consistently measure up.

Lack and Measuring Up

Experiencing lack has a way of making you feel as if self is at the very center of every equation in our lives. Jesus, on the other hand, should always remain our primary focus. The problem is that we're so consumed with feeling less than, left out, and unable to measure up to other people's standards that we forfeit the joy we obtain through our relationship with

Christ. In fact, many of us, due to our past childhood experiences (maybe many adult ones as well), believe God also has an orange measuring stick. We picture a mean God who is always in a bad mood, constantly measuring our submission, our commitment, and our religious performance. I used to believe He might use that yardstick to smack me with whenever I got out of line. This is because I had a distorted view of God. Even though I had been taught in church about God's unconditional love, I really didn't understand it. Even as an adult when my pastor would teach about God's grace, I still felt condemned because I didn't believe I measured up to the "holiness" standard. This standard was one that was expected by man, not of God. My problem was that I didn't fully know God's heart toward me nor did I understand the wonderful attributes of His divine grace. If I had understood His grace, I would know that I could run to Him no matter what my "bad"was, and He would unconditionally love me and accept me. His mercy was already ready to receive me and His grace was available, at all times, to empower me to move forward and fulfill my destiny in Christ.

Now, back to lack and how it is connected to our need to measure up. As long as you believe that you have to measure up and perform properly to please others, you will suffer with a sense of emptiness and lack. It's a never ending road that keeps you jumping through hoops your entire life. If we choose to bow down to lack, it is the same as committing idolatry. All too often we believe God is deliberately withholding His best from us, and the result is that we believe a lie concerning God.

God is a good God. Jeremiah 29:11 tells us that He has a plan for our lives, and it is to give us a hope and a great future. As sons and daughters, we have a heavenly inheritance that identifies us as King's kids and of His royal blood. Philippians 4:19 reminds us that "it is he who will supply all your needs from his riches in glory because of what Christ Jesus has done for us" (TLB). Jesus Himself said, "My purpose is to give life in all its fullness" (John 10:10, TLB). Yet for so many of us, we remain on the treadmill of introspection and frustration, and we suffer from feelings of inadequacy and insecurity.

Dear one, there is a way out of this pattern! I have good news for you: you don't have to remain in this cycle! It is my heart to provide God's truths that will inspire you to experience that full life that Jesus has promised. I believe that as you read, the Holy Spirit is ministering to your spirit and is supernaturally transforming your life as your minds are being renewed to His truth! So keep reading-greater freedom and breakthrough awaits you!

The Genesis of Lack

Ever since the Garden of Eden, mankind has been cycling through life with a sense of lack. It came with a subtle seduction. Satan beguiled Eve with his sly suggestions that targeted Eve's identity. He also planted a seed of doubt by suggesting God's desire to withhold His best from her. Remember, satan did not come right out and misrepresent God to Eve. Neither did he lay out his plans of destruction up front. He slyly interjected the thought that God did not want her to eat of both trees in the Garden of Eden, knowing that this would cause Eve to believe she was being "left out" and kept from something good. The bait of satan was to get Eve to believe that God was withholding His best from her. Then, He connected her with a sense of lack again by suggesting that

God did not want her to be like Him. What a deception! Eve was created in the image of God; *she was already like Him*!

When God created man, he was made in the image of God and was given dominion and was called "blessed" (see Genesis 1:26-30). Imagine how much He loved what He had created. He gave Adam and Eve authority to rule in His kingdom! They had every blessing imaginable promised to them; there was no such thing as lack.

A sense of lack hooks us. Think about it. Advertisers know how to capitalize on lack through subtle suggestions that we "need" their product. And, if we don't purchase it, we will be "less than." Many of us might even blame God because he hasn't given us that "thing" that we "desperately" need! Political campaigns also capitalize on the sense of lack. Each party presents our nation as "needy." We soon believe we "need" a new president or a new political representative to help with the "needs" of the nation. Their campaigns fill our hearts and minds with fear. Soon torment takes over and we find ourselves making hasty decisions. We have now looked to man to be a solution rather than to seek God for His divine direction.

Satan started off by asking Eve a few questions. He starts off the same with us; he questions us concerning the faithfulness of God. He questions God's acceptance of us. Unfortunately, the church at large often presents the same type of questions. In church, "terroristic" preachers place fear and terror in the hearts and minds of God's children. Pulpit messages that demand religious performance, obeying rules, and doctrines of man keep us busy *doing* rather than simply *being*. Bad theology has replaced God's perfect love in our minds. We have been threatened with God's inability to accept us unless we do all the right things rather than allow His perfect love to drive away all the fears of never measuring up and suffering lack.

1 John 4:18-19 is a very important passage that we need to keep at the forefront of our minds throughout this chapter; it says, "There is no fear in love; but perfect love casts out fear, because fear involves punishment, and the one who fears is not perfected in love. We love, because He first loved us" (NASB).

Believer, this passage means that it is God's love for us that will drive out fear. There is no way for us to be perfect in love. This passage is referring to God's perfect love for us that promises to drive away our fears. What fears? The fear of punishment that might occur if we don't measure up. Or, the fear that we've messed up so much that God will withhold His best from us, and we will be plagued with lack. No! Christ went to the cross to put us eternally in right-standing with God. We are righteous in Christ. The word *righteous* means right standing. There is nothing we can do within ourselves (no good works, religious deeds, obeying the Ten Commandments, praying hour upon hour, or being in church every Sunday!) that makes us holy or righteous. We are holy because Christ is holy. We are righteous only because Christ is righteous.

Again, the church has been trained to suggest that we need to measure up to a particular standard to be acceptable to God. The church has several yard sticks. I know at one time I had one of those when I ministered as a local pastor. Yes, I wrongly believed that it was my responsibility to keep the sheep walking the straight line. I taught on holiness so much that people didn't believe they were holy enough to attend church!

I asked all the wrong questions as a pastor. I would preach and teach in a way that caused others to question whether or not they were "good" enough for God to love or bless them. I asked people, "Are you praying enough-like every day- or better yet almost all day?" I asked, "Where's your commitment in God? Are you serving in the nursery? Are you studying the Word *daily*? Are you....." The questions were endless. They were not *direct* questions, but as ministers, we often have a way of causing people to feel guilty for not "doing" enough. The bottom line is that this behavior is control and manipulation. As New Covenant ministers, we should build up the confidence of who the saints are in Christ rather than shame them into religious performance. Remember, shame promotes a feeling of lack. For instance, if we lack money to buy suitable clothing or a nice house, we feel "ashamed." Thus, once again, our true identity is challenged. Failure to "have," "be," "know," "do"...the list goes on and on...targets each of our identities every day. Unfortunately, to control the flock, preachers have preached sin-consciousness messages for decades. Messages that target our "need to be better" are preached to keep the congregation coming back to church. Why? They are *never* able to measure up to the Law of the Old Covenant, tradition, and the doctrines of man. To be more specific, rather than focusing on the "Don't-er-onomies," begin to focus on the "Do-ter-onomies!" (referring to the book of Deuteronomy, of course).

I realize today that much of my ministry in the past was done from a sin-consciousness belief system. The expectations I had for myself and others would always involve the need to be better, do more, and measure up to a new level. My heart was right, but my focus was entirely wrong. You see, I needed for people to "act right" so that I felt as if I were doing a good job. To be completely honest, I was afraid of failure which fueled my need to control. How did I control? Through messages that promoted shame, guilt, and condemnation. Basically, I was attempting to be the Holy Spirit by continually convicting others of sin. I lacked confidence in myself and in God. This type of ministry from me or anyone is based upon the presumption of lack and the need for performance.

No More Condemnation!

> There is therefore now no condemnation to them that are in Christ Jesus. For the law of the Spirit of life in Christ Jesus made me free from the law of sin and of death. For what the law could not do, in that it was weak through the flesh, God, sending his own Son in the likeness of sinful flesh and for sin, condemned sin in the flesh: that the ordinance of the law might be fulfilled in us, who walk not after the flesh, but after the Spirit (Romans 8:1-4, ASV).

As we ponder Romans 8:1, we recognize the burden apostle Paul must have felt concerning us, as believers, to realize that there is no condemnation for those who are in Christ. Dear ones, it's plainly stated that we are no longer condemned if we have been born again. Paul says that a New Covenant believer is no longer under the Old Testament Law of sin and death, but rather submitted to a new law of the Spirit of life! Think about this: when we are born again, we are under a new law where we are legally given the gift of eternal life! Paul goes on to state that God sent Jesus as the ultimate sacrifice for sin to enable us to walk after the Spirit; the Law could not do this for us because it was weak through the flesh.

The Old Covenant was the Jewish law that God gave to Israel. It consisted of over 600 do's and don'ts (there's those

Don't-er-nomies popping up again!). Scripture is very clear that the Law never saved anyone (see Romans 3:20 and Galatians 2:16). The Law was intended only as a shadow, painting a picture of Jesus Christ to come. It is true that multitudes looked to the Law for the hope of their salvation, but ultimately they realized that the Law would only bring death and condemnation (see 2 Corinthians 3:7).

Believers are no longer under the Old Covenant Law. The law, today, serves as an instrument for *un*believers. How is that? Because the Law makes us aware of our sin problems (see 1 Timothy 1:8-11 and Romans 3:19-20). Within ourselves, we cannot fulfill the perfect standards of the Law. It's clear in Galatians 3:21-22 that we will always "fall short" meaning that we *fail* in our attempts to fulfill the Law.

> For if a law had been given that could impart life, then righteousness would certainly have come by the law. But Scripture has locked up everything under the control of sin, so that what was promised, being given through faith in Jesus Christ, might be given to those who believe (Galatians 3:21b-22).

Precious believer, the Law cannot encourage us. The Law will *never* praise us. Neither will tradition or religious doctrine. This is why religious performance will ultimately end up condemning us; we'll never measure up!

Still Feeling Guilty?

Still not convinced that you'll survive without performing properly for God and man? Let's take this subject just one step further. Interestingly, the word *condemnation* means "a verdict or a type of judgment (i.e.; a court trial and found guilty needing sentencing with a type of punishment)." Did you notice the key words *guilty* and *punishment*? Isn't it true that when we fall short or fail, we expect to be condemned or punished? In other words, because we've messed up, we need to be punished. When we are punished, something ends up being taken away or there is suffering involved. Result? We experience an ongoing sense of lack. It's easy to understand this cycle if you've ever felt condemned.

So many believers, and I was one of these, are afraid of punishment from God so you withdraw from God rather than run to Him. Shame causes us to respond that way, doesn't it? But God encourages us to run to Him for divine empowerment through His abundant grace.

Again, Paul makes it clear to us as he writes that God did not punish him for failing to measure up to certain standards—especially religious standards! He was reminding us of that same fact when he wrote to the church in Rome. Let me remind you that the book of Romans is considered by theologians to be Paul's greatest work; it is placed first among his thirteen epistles in the New Testament. This wonderful book explores the significance of Christ's sacrificial death; this is a revelation we all need to understand of how good God is and how much He truly loves us!

I recommend that you take some private time and study the entire book of Romans. If you do, you will notice the question and answer format as Paul presents practical exhortation that is considered the Good News to us. Questions that Paul uses exhort rather than condemn. The questions that he presents in the book of Romans edifies rather than deflates. I would have loved to sit under him as a pastor!

Paul presents the good news of Jesus Christ as more than mere facts, but explains clearly that the fullness of life due to Christ is available to us. Let's observe more closely what he writes: "For all have sinned and fall short of the glory of God, and are *justified freely by his grace* through the redemption that came by Christ Jesus" (Romans 3:23-24, emphasis added).

There are two important truths that we each need to understand if we desire experience the fullness of life which is *only* available through the finished work of Christ Jesus on the cross:

1. **We are freely justified by grace.**
   Remember, Romans 3:24 states that we are "justified freely by his grace." When we search out the full meaning of justification, we realize that justification is God's declaration that the demands of His Law have been fulfilled *only* in the righteousness of His Son and His death on the cross. Paul tells us that we are reconciled to the Father due to the offering of the blood of Jesus (see Hebrews 10:14, Romans 5:9). Believer, when God justifies, He charges the sin of mankind to Christ. He then credits the righteousness of Christ to the believer and we can stand before God "just-as-if I'd- never sinned! "(see 2 Corinthians 5:21, Romans 5:18). God is therefore "just" because His holy standard of perfect righteousness has been completely fulfilled in Christ. Believer, it's important that we allow this to sink deep into your heart and spirit: according to Romans 3:26 and 5:16, this righteousness is *freely given* to every believer. I am praying for you as I write because I want you completely set free from all self-righteousness and religious performance. I pray you are

as excited as I was when God revealed this truth to my heart. This is revelation that will set you free from all fears of not being able to "measure up."

2. **We receive this justification which is freely given to us through** *faith.*
Although the Lord Jesus paid the complete price for our justification, it is through our faith that we receive His righteousness. Dear one, every time the enemy attempts to speak lies to you and say that you are shameful, unworthy, or that you just can't seem to "measure up" to a holy standard, rise up in faith and remind that devil that you are justified and righteous due to the blood of Jesus! In fact, think about this for a minute: according to Romans 4:3, 9 faith is considered righteousness not because of the works of man, but due to the gift and work of God! (John 6:28-29, Galatians 2:16).

A New Creation

Therefore if any person is [ingrafted] in Christ (the Messiah) he is a new creation (a new creature altogether); the old [previous moral and spiritual condition] has passed away. Behold, the fresh and new has come! (2 Corinthians 5:17, AMP).

> WE ARE NO LONGER SLAVES TO SIN BECAUSE WE NO LONGER HAVE A SIN NATURE.

A divine shift needs to occur within the hearts of God's children. This shift involves renewing our minds to the truth that we are dead to sin; we are a new creation in Christ. This means we have a new nature. We are no longer slaves to sin because we no longer have a sin nature. No longer are we sin-conscious, but rather righteousness conscious! We need to be continually reminded that we are to "put off the old man," and then "put on the new!"

Read another passage from the apostle Paul that will enlighten you concerning being dead to sin and its enslavement:

> In the same way, count yourselves dead to sin but alive to God in Christ Jesus. Therefore do not let sin reign in your mortal body so that you obey its evil desires. Do not offer the parts of your body to sin, as instruments of wickedness, but rather offer yourselves to God, as those who have been brought from death to life; and offer the parts of your body to him as instruments of righteousness. For sin shall not be your master, because you are not under law, but under grace (Romans 6:11-14).

Make A Declaration!

It's important for us to periodically stand up and boldly declare out loud, "I am dead to sin! I am alive in Christ. Christ lives in me. The Holy Spirit dwells in me, the temple of God. I am a new creation, the old is passed away and the new is here...now!" If we continually remind ourselves of our identity in Christ we will be endued with power to overcome all of the lies of the enemy. Remember, the accuser will attempt to remind you of your past, but you are moving past your past! That's why this book will prove powerful in your life; it reminds you that you are not what you "do" that brings fulfillment, but rather "who" and "whose" you are!

It's unfortunate that, due to all of the misunderstood messages in the Word, we have distorted views of God. We don't know how to embrace His love due to our past upbringing or teaching. Unless we renew our minds concerning the depth of love God has for us, we will continually believe we fall short of deserving His love.

I have spent the last several years studying about the unconditional love of God. It was difficult for me to comprehend due to my childhood. I loved my parents, but they were extremely strict. I had to walk a straight line and perform to feel loved. I was rewarded when I pleased them. So I learned at a very early age the need to perform to feel loved. It was the same in my relationship with God for many, many years.

We all have been on the same journey—I'm quite sure of it. But rather than remain in blame mode and pointing the finger at others who may have helped to mold me into a religious misfit, I made a decision to take responsibility for my own actions. It is our individual responsibility to seek God and His truths concerning His goodness, His righteousness, and His desire to bless us. I am writing to help you understand those concepts, but you, precious child of God, must also call out to Him, seek Him out, and ask the Holy Spirit to guide you into all truth. Never allow any one person in your life to be the sole voice of instruction concerning God and the Scripture. It is your responsibility to maintain an intimate relationship with your Father and to continually ask for the Holy Spirit to lead you. Always try to remember this very important statement: **The Holy Spirit is your teacher** and not your circumstance, your past, your storm, or your tests. Those things are your experiences that involve overcoming. The Holy Spirit guides you through those trials and experiences, and His voice teaches you the truth concerning all of those areas. So, why not choose to let go of our religious mindsets and simply crawl into the lap of God and let Him love on you a bit?

We Are Complete in Christ!

Let me conclude this chapter with an additional important statement: **You are complete in Christ**. Our sense of being complete is rooted in our understanding that we are complete in Jesus. It is not what we do; it's what He already did! If that understanding does not become foundational, every question we ask ourselves is acted out through a vicious cycle of experiencing a sense of lack and attempting to measure up through religion and dead works. Dear one, there is no victory in that cycle.

To believe that we are responsible for completeness is a lie from satan. Eve took his bait. She believed that there was something God was withholding from her, and therefore, alienated herself from God. She abandoned her promise of blessing, power, and life that provided the opportunity to live in the Garden. The very instant she believed the lie concerning lack, she exchanged her faith in God and believing He was good for fear and torment. What satan deceived her into first believing became a fact, and she experienced lack because she believed God was withholding from her. She basically received what she was seduced into believing.

If we continue to believe the lies of the enemy, we will remain in vicious cycles that steal or abort our destiny. Failure has many masks. The failure to measure up brings a sense of lack, shame, guilt, and even condemnation. Maybe you have noticed that with any sense of failure, there is shame and guilt attached. The Lord has set you free from all shame and guilt. It is my prayer that you can let go of it now. However, the enemy's plan to keep you in a place of hopelessness can be defeated along Freedom Road—the road we travel together! If you can identify with a particular cycle, allow your faith to rise! It's time to break any cycle that links us to past behaviors and false belief systems; yet, for now you can also conclude with me that these feelings, actions, and beliefs are intertwined.

We will never break out of these deadly cycles unless we turn back to God and His truth. All of Paul's writings were written with the primary focus to teach God's children to understand the power in the finished work of Christ. At the cross, our identity in God was established, our righteousness was established, and our victory in life was settled once and forever. We are victorious overcomers because of the word of our testimony and the blood of the Lamb. Believer, I want to encourage you to read my recent book entitled, ***Power in the Blood of Jesus: Claiming Your Spiritual Inheritance*** (Chosen Books, 2013). I have written in great detail what was accomplished at the cross and the power that we have when we understand that we have a royal inheritance because of Christ's ultimate sacrifice.

In the closing of this chapter, I wish to refer back to Paul's teachings. Once you understand that your entire sense of wholeness and completeness is based upon the finished work of Jesus at the cross, you are empowered to stand firm and not waver in your identity. You are righteous because Jesus died for you. What was accomplished at the cross settled the debt of all your sin. Everything you will ever need in life is provided for you because Christ already paid the price for it. You can stand upon that rock of truth because Jesus is the Rock!

Understanding the grace of God is foundational if you have experienced failure. To me, God's grace not only involves unconditional love, but also unconditional forgiveness. Yes, I believe He forgives unconditionally. You see, we will *never* be perfect as long as we live in these fleshly bodies. "Sin" in Greek is the word *hamartano*, and it basically means not only to err, but also to "miss the mark." I guess that would fit with my perception of not measuring up, right? As we walk out our lives and learn more how to depend on the Spirit of God rather than the arm of the flesh, He will be faithful to point out where we might go sideways. The Holy Spirit will teach us how to walk by His principles that lead to the Tree of Life so that we don't fulfill the lust of the flesh (see Galatians 5:16). It's our responsibility to cooperate with His grace. The way that we know if we are cooperating is to examine our fruit. Taking time to do a spiritual fruit examination is vital whenever we are learning to walk in His grace. Otherwise, we might too easily cast caution to the wind and embrace any temptation that satan hurls our way. Believer, you are well on your way to understanding the goodness of God! Let's take some time now to reflect on what you've learned.

Believer, I am so very proud of you! Do you realize that once you began to read the very first paragraph of this book that you were already beginning to renew your mind? Isn't that exciting? You see, it's not about what you do right; it's all about the Holy Spirit leading you and guiding you into all truth. By reading this book, the Holy Spirit is teaching you biblical truth, and at the same time your mind is being renewed. All you need to do is rest in His ability to transform you as you follow His Spirit.

Now, let's continue to move forward. Don't forget to grab your pen or pencil just in case you wish to write some comments in the margins. Or, even use the highlighter as the Holy Spirit prompts. It's important to listen to His voice as we continue this journey.

A Time of Reflection

Do you experience the joy of wholeness or is there a continual foreboding feeling of lack? Maybe you are not sure just what you feel at this point. Could it be that you are simply burned out from performance? Maybe you've jumped too high and through too many hoops, and you found yourself still lacking and needing even more approval.

Allow me to help you by suggesting a simple exercise that may help you find a solution:

1.   Get alone with God. Be sure to have your Bible, a journal or paper, and a pen or pencil.

2.   Do a Scripture search and pick out a few verses that speak about being complete in Christ. If you have a **Strong's Exhaustive Concordance**, it will help you locate several of them.

3.   Allow the Holy Spirit to speak to you as you read them. The passages that minister to you should then be written down.

4.   As you meditate on Scripture, begin to picture yourself completed in Christ. See yourself as an overcomer, conquering any sense of lack, doubt, unworthiness, or the failure of not measuring up. As you meditate, let go of all bitterness that might arise. The Holy Spirit may have you forgive someone that He brings to your mind as you are meditating.

5.   Next, after documenting Scriptures and meditating, begin to quote the passages aloud. This is similar to making a decree over your life. A decree will empower you to cycle out of the enemy's plans of destruction as you will read about in the next chapter.

6. Think about inserting your name where applicable as you speak and speak the verses in present tense. This will personalize it for you and speaking in present tense activates hope.

    To whom God willed to make known what is the riches of the glory of this mystery among the Gentiles, which is Christ in you, the hope of glory. And we proclaim Him, admonishing every man and teaching every man with all wisdom, that we may present every man *complete* in Christ (Colossians 1:27-28, NASB, emphasis added).

    In this passage, you would insert your name once more and decree it in present tense as if it were part of your belief system NOW! Let me show you an example once more:

    "To Sandie Freed, God wills to make known to Sandie Freed what are the riches of the glory of this mystery...which is Christ in Sandie Freed, the hope of glory. And Sandie Freed proclaims Him, and is presented as complete in Christ."

CHAPTER 7

When Doing Your Best is Never Enough

"I just can't do this anymore! I feel as if I am literally
going to die. I've done my best at pastoring
and it is still not good enough. I've done my best at
being holy and it is not good enough!"

This was me...crying out to my husband, Mickey... just before we stopped pastoring a local church in Bedford, Texas. We had pastored there for fourteen years-from 1990 to 2004. I want you to know up-front that I have pastored the most loving people, and I can honestly write that I had a genuine pastoral love for each of them. Still, hurting people hurt people and sometimes when many hurting and needy people are in your congregation, it can be a challenge. Yet, I have always loved the challenge of helping people become successful and transform. Also, you need to know that it was never about the people having to perform to my expectations—it was all about the need in me to feel successful.

The words I quoted earlier to my husband were becoming all too familiar to him. He had heard them over and over for almost a year. It was one of the hardest seasons in my life. I had several other seasons when I was challenged, and I didn't help lead our local flock. One of them was when I had an eating disorder and almost died from a heart attack at the age of twenty-seven. You can read my entire testimony in my book *Dream On: Unlocking Your Dreams and Visions* (Zion Ministries, 6th edition, 2011). Another one was when I was barely over thirty and I almost died from a viral infection. God had miraculously saved my life, healed my body, and delivered me from bondage and the jaws of death. But now, in this season of pastoring a church, I just could not hang on any longer. I wanted OUT!

Ministering to our people in the earlier years of my life was always difficult. There were several challenges I could not overcome and that meant failure to me. I believed the lie that I was a failure in ministry because we were not a mega-sized church. After all, successful pastors had large congregations—at least that is what I believed. Also, I didn't understand why I couldn't be like so many others in ministry who seemed to overcome sheep bites. I kept getting encouraging words from others who would say, "Sandie, God is going to give you duck feathers. When the rains come, the problems of the storm will just roll off of you like they roll off duck feathers." Well, the duck feathers never grew. Nothing rolled off of me; I took everything too personally. Now, I know why. My struggle in ministry (or in business, marriages, relationships—well, and life in general!) is not an isolated one! Many believers continually struggle with self-righteousness versus God's righteousness. To understand what I am trying to point out we need to look closely at each one:

Self-righteousness is our own attempt and effort to achieve recognition, love and acceptance by God. It is we, as human individuals, attempting to fulfill God's Word through deeds (works) of righteousness and through our own strength in order to relieve ourselves from guilt and the penalty of sin.

God's righteousness is God's gift to us. This gift is imputed to each of us through the death and resurrection of His sinless Son, Jesus Christ. Jesus chose the cross, to carry our sin to that cross at Calvary. In doing so, He put all of us in right standing with Himself. Jesus Christ became the eternal sacrifice; He made is as if sin never existed.

In my recent book, ***Power in the Blood: Claiming Your Spiritual Inheritance*** (Chosen Books, 2007, 2013), I talk about this subject in great detail. One of my favorite teachings concerns the justification we received because of what Jesus did at Calvary. We briefly touched on this subject in the last chapter. Justification is similar to a legal action in a court of law where someone is referred to as "just." God has legally declared us just and righteous! And, then, we are treated and looked upon as someone who can therefore say, "It's just as if I'd never sinned!" Justified!

Israel's Failures

When we examine Romans 10:2-3, we read that all the while that Israel was serving God; they truly believed in their hearts that they were being established in God by their own righteousness:

> For I can testify about them that they are zealous for God, but their zeal is not based on knowledge. Since they did not know the righteousness that comes from God and sought to establish their own, they did not submit to God's righteousness. Christ is the end of the law so that there may be righteousness for everyone who believes (Romans 10:2-4).

Here we see the deception of man's own ideas concerning righteousness. Unfortunately, this is still a major issue in the church. Quite often when failure is experienced, we divert to a previous type of performance in an attempt to twist God's arm so that He might bless us and forgive us because we have fallen short. I have realized that I don't have to convince God to bless me or to heal me. Provision and healing were provided through *sozo* and the finished work of Jesus.

Man's religion demands that we measure up, use human effort and energy (even manipulate if we have to!) to get God's attention and favor. But, let me assure you, there is nothing we can do within ourselves to become righteous. It is a gift!

When we get to the end of ourselves, sometimes we are more open to hear the truth concerning this concept. I thought I understood the difference between self-righteousness and God's righteousness. However, the bottom line was that I didn't.

I still like to look at the life of Abraham, the father of our faith (read more about his great faith in Hebrews 11:8-11) from time to time as it continually encourages me. I realize that we have already discussed Abraham in a previous chapter but allow me to remind you what the Word says concerning Abraham's *faith*. Romans 4:1-3 states that Abraham's faith was NOT justified by works, but by faith. It was his faith in God's righteousness that made Him righteous!

> What then shall we say that Abraham, our forefather according to the flesh, discovered in this matter? If, in fact, Abraham was justified by works, he had something to boast about—but not before God. What does the Scripture say? "Abraham believed

God, and it was credited to him as righteousness"
(Romans 4:1-3).

I know I am hammering this truth that our
righteousness is in Christ, but I am doing so because it is
foundational to rising up after any type of failure. Remember:
insecurity, inferiority, fear of failure, loss, grief, etc. can be
translated as "failing to measure up" to our expectations or
God's expectations! So believer, believe in what Christ
accomplished at the cross; He has made you completely 100%
righteous!

How a Self-Righteous Person Thinks

Allow me to share what a self-righteous person thinks
about righteousness. Lists from others in various professions
would be similar. I can to this with all sincerity because these
were some of my own thoughts: I'm holier and more righteous
than others because I...

- go to church more than others.
- am a pastor of a local church.
- am a minister of the gospel.
- pray more than others.
- study the Word more than others.
- tithe 15% rather than 10%.
- tithe period!
- don't wear jeans or slacks in the pulpit.
- don't wear flip flops in the pulpit.
- don't dance in church.
- pray in the Spirit at least 30 minutes a day.
- never, ever, go barefoot in church (even when your
  feet hurt).

The list of righteous deeds goes on and on and on. The emphasis is "I" and not "Him." I can remember believing that if I wore slacks (jeans were completely out of the question) when I ministered that I would appear to others as unholy. Of course, I also believe that it would have offended God and He would disapprove! It was as if I believed it would rob me of the anointing. Jeepers! I used to believe that you couldn't dance in church, laugh in church, or have fun in church. The deception of such a belief system kept me in religious bondage. Yes, I was yoked to self-righteousness, and that type of yoke is plain and simple: PRIDE. Ouch! Jesus addressed the Pharisees, teaching them that it was what was in the heart of a man that defiled him. Their strict observance of hand washing could not make them righteous or holy before the Lord (see Matthew 15:15-20). Aren't you glad that you are free from the Law and religious performance?

Having correct motives will empower us to see God's righteousness over self-righteousness. It matters not only *what we do for God*, but *why we do for God*. Do we get busy for Him because we believe we get extra credit? Maybe He will love and bless us more if we serve? Or do we serve because the Holy Spirit is leading us, and we have a heart to remain obedient?

Most of us have experienced the "crabby Christian syndrome." This is when you take a bunch of Christian crabs and put them in a large bucket. Christian Crab #1 climbs to the top and Crab #2 climbs up and pulls him down. Guess what? When Crab#2 climbs up to get out, there's Christian Crab 3, 4, and 5 waiting in line. In other words, no one makes it completely to the top! Why? Jealousy, envy, strife, self-righteousness, and "me, me, me" and "I, I, I" syndromes.

I can hear you asking, "What does this have to do with failure?" If you will recall, all the Israelites died in the wilderness, with the exception of Joshua and Caleb. God waited until an entire generation died before He took the next group into the Promised Land. Talk about feeling like a failure? The ten spies who returned from Canaan with a negative report failed to see God's goodness and His faithfulness to fulfill His promises. Joshua and Caleb were the only two spies who returned to Moses with a positive report, believing that Israel was well-able to move forward and take possession of their land of promise. Yet, Joshua, representing a new generation of faithful believers, was chosen by God to lead Israel into their Promised Land.

I believe with my whole heart that Joshua and Caleb gave it their best shot to convince Israel that they were well—able to take the land. Yet, their best just wasn't good enough. Israel was too steeped in focusing on their own human abilities—and their faith failed them. They saw themselves as grasshoppers, rather than God's conquerors. They were focused on their own abilities rather than God's promises. If they could have trusted in the righteousness and holiness of a faithful God, I believe they could have risen up with great faith and taken their land!

Joshua had at least forty years to ponder the failures of Israel and even the failure of Moses. When it was his time to lead, I believe that he knew that he could not take their promised territory in his own strength and effort. **God chose Joshua because He could trust Joshua to trust Him!** After all, the crossing of the Jordan was supernatural; Joshua had nothing to do with walking across the river on dry land. How about Jericho? Was it the marching that caused the walls to tumble? Was it their shout? No, it was in their following the voice of God—remaining obedient and trusting in His ability to give them their victory! This proves that victory comes through His righteousness. Yes, we experience right-standing and righteousness through Jesus' death and resurrection; He paid the price for us to have His righteousness. However, we receive this righteousness by using our faith and confessing the Word (see Romans 10:9-10). Remember, *sozo* is the result of the finished work of the cross. Therefore, no matter what battle we are in, we fight "from" the victory established at the cross and not "to" the victory. Paul reminds us that when Christ went to the cross, died, and was resurrected, "[God] disarmed the principalities and powers that were ranged against us and made a bold display and public example of them, in triumphing over them in Him and in it [the cross]" (Colossians 2:15, AMP). Yes, the enemy is already defeated on your behalf! Our responsibility is simply to believe and receive.

Zealous for God

It's good to be zealous for God, but not with the wrong motive. I recently wrote about Elijah and how he had great zeal for God. Yet, he saw himself as "I alone" am zealous to serve God. Elijah had become a loner, so to speak. And, in his loneliness I believe he felt like a failure when he was running away from Queen Jezebel. Whenever we believe that "we alone" are left to do the work of the Kingdom; well, let me just say it's a dangerous place to be. How do I know? Remember I am writing a lot from personal experience in this chapter. I felt as "I alone" was holy because I did not sin—or at least I thought I didn't. I forgot about jealousy, envy, coveting, and desiring something out of God's timing. Just my believing I was holy due to my own righteousness was the wrong belief system! And just like Elijah, I was caught up completely in my own self-righteousness. Ugh!

As a "holier than thou" preacher, it seemed as if I remained frustrated with God's people because I couldn't get them all into the Holy of Holies! I would get phone calls or emails concerning the behavior of others and then preach another "terrorist" sermon attempting to shame them into obedience and holiness. Is it any wonder I eventually wore myself out? And, God, in His divine grace, knew I wasn't going to get much further in ministry with an attitude like that. So, He released me from pastoring to ten years of traveling ministry in which I wrote twelve books. Yes, there was a lot in me waiting to be released! However, over the years, though, I have ministered to hundreds of frustrated pastors who are experiencing the same burn out. I really believed that I had an isolated problem, but I was alarmingly wrong. It is a dilemma I witness almost everywhere I travel. What again is the dilemma? It is the challenge within each of our religious egos that negates the revelation that it's never good enough when we depend upon our own strength and self-righteousness.

Unfortunately, sometimes our zeal for God is of an impure motive. Sadly, I have to admit, that in the beginning phases of my personal ministry, it was very important for me to appear successful. Yet it has taken me years to understand God's principles of success. I have realized that I really can't figure it all out—His ladder to success. All that I know is that it is a dichotomy: the way up is down. The least is the greatest in the Kingdom. To die is to live. My personal journey has been that which I have stated. I am learning to be content with little, and I know God recognizes me even if there is no recognition elsewhere. My success is all wrapped up in pleasing Him. I'm not indicating that I'm totally there yet, but I definitely remind myself who I am in Him when I feel like a failure!

There are several other people in Scripture that are noted as being zealous for God. Many of the disciples are noted as having zeal—especially Peter. Jehu also was zealous (see 2 Kings 10:17), and his zeal for God involved ending the illegitimate reign of the wife of King Ahab, Jezebel. It seemed to be easy for Jehu to be zealous. He gets anointed and then grabs people by the hand along the way to ride in his chariot as he fulfills his divine mission. How fun is that? Thinking back, I only had a handful that desired to be grabbed as I fulfilled my mission. Did you get that? *My* mission? Yep, that was the barricade: my barrier and shut down point. "I" didn't have a mission...I was always on "His" mission. I can fulfill my destiny only through His unmerited favor, due to His grace.

I wish I could testify that I have had all pure motives in my past. Pure motives meaning that I didn't care if I was successful in what I did for the Lord. But according to this new revelation concerning God's righteousness, I fell short—very short! However, now that I know let me just say to you that I have moved past previous condemnation and remind myself to put off the old man and put on the new! Why am I telling you this? Because I believe that you can learn from my challenges; you can be a champion; you can overcome past failures and fears of failure...and achieve your destiny in God. And, dear one, that is exactly why I write to you now in order to challenge you to be an overcomer and succeed in God! When you realize that Jesus has already paid the price for you to experience the fullness of life, you will begin to rejoice with me.

Change

God does not require that we change first in order that we become more "right" with Him. No way! Remember this always: when you accept Jesus as your personal Savior you are immediately in right standing with Him. It is all about our understanding this truth that changes us! This is what I often refer to as effortless change. It is, therefore, God's responsibility to lead us and teach us to do good works and guide us as we live a life of holiness unto Him. However, our past sin consciousness will always desire to rise up and take control. Precious ones, we must resist that temptation! If we do not fully believe that what Jesus accomplished at the cross will transform us, then we negate His sacrifice for our sins. If we have believed wrongly concerning our righteousness in Christ, then simply repent and move on. Remember, repentance means to change the way we think. Therefore, repentance is needed as we renew our minds. Believer, stay with me. Let your faith arise as you continue to read.

Apostle Paul continually challenged religious mindsets concerning strict adherence to the Law. We will look at how the Law shuts up faith in a later chapter, but for now I want you to see how Paul viewed the act of circumcision which was part of the Law. The reason for his addressing the Law concerning circumcision was because of Peter. Bless his heart; he really tried to do everything right! But even his best efforts were not enough. If you recall his story, Peter believed that the Gentiles needed to be circumcised. Peter needed some instruction concerning the grace of God and the finished work of Christ so Paul corrected Peter's belief system. Notice in the passage below that Paul says that we are "free" from the "yoke" of bondage to the Law. And, also that if we remain obedient to the Law, we are therefore alienated from Christ which means that what Christ did at the cross was to no avail to set us completely free:

> It is for freedom that Christ has set us free. Stand firm, then, and do not let yourselves be burdened again by a yoke of slavery. Mark my words! I, Paul, tell you that if you let yourselves be circumcised, Christ will be of no value to you at all. Again I declare to every man who lets himself be circumcised that he is obligated to obey the whole law. You who are trying to be justified by law have been alienated from Christ; you have fallen away from grace. For through the Spirit we eagerly await by faith the righteousness for which we hope. For in Christ Jesus neither circumcision nor uncircumcision has any value. The only thing that counts is faith expressing itself through love (Galatians 5:1-6).

Again, our *very best efforts in our self-righteous acts are never good enough!* As apostle Paul reminds us, the only thing that has any value is our "faith expressing itself through love (in God!)" (Galatians 5:6, expanded by author).

> IT'S GOD'S RIGHTEOUSNESS THAT EMPOWERS US TO LIVE A HOLY LIFE AND TO DO GOOD WORKS.

So, how do we change our minds, our lives, our lifestyles, and our behavior? The answer is so very simple, yet we make it so hard. It's almost too good to be true, but it is both good and true! It is God's righteousness that empowers us to live a holy life and to do good works. We can't act right to be righteous; we need to believe right! We become righteous through Christ and then do right. When we realize we are already in right

148

standing with God, we will emanate the life of Jesus, who is already in Heaven seated at the right hand of the Father. Colossians 3:1 states this in the Amplified Version: "IF THEN you have been raised with Christ [to a new life, thus sharing His resurrection from the dead], aim at and seek the [rich, eternal treasures] that are above, where Christ is, seated at the right hand of God."

Yes, we have a *new life*, and we share His resurrection power. We are encouraged to aim at and seek eternal treasures which I believe are all the blessings that come from *sozo*. Having a new life means that we are no longer sinners saved by grace, and therefore, still destined to keep sinning. No! We are now clothed with the righteousness of Christ and empowered to live a holy life...all because of His finished work at the cross.

However, the devil does not take a nap whenever you are on the road to discovering who you *really* are! He will target those fiery darts your way to tempt you into stumbling. To wage war against the enemy without taking the posture of a son is futile. However knowing who you are in Christ and the finished work at Calvary will defeat him in the battle every time. Dear one, remember this one thing: **you fight *from* the victory and not *to* the victory!** Wage war from the victory at the cross, and the devil doesn't stand a chance.

We must always keep this thought at the forefront of our minds: **we are no longer guided by our flesh when we become born-again**. Once we receive salvation *(sozo)*, we become sons and daughters of God led by the Holy Spirit. When we begin to walk in the Spirit of God we are empowered to overcome the lusts of the flesh. Read the following passage carefully and notice that when we are led by the Spirit we are no longer subject to the Law (which is connected to OUR trying to do our best through self-righteousness).

> But I say, walk and live [habitually] in the [Holy] Spirit [responsive to and controlled and guided by the Spirit]; then you will certainly not gratify the cravings and desires of the flesh (of human nature without God). For the desires of the flesh are opposed to the [Holy] Spirit, and the [desires of the] Spirit are opposed to the flesh (godless human nature); for these are antagonistic to each other [continually withstanding and in conflict with each other], so that you are not free but are prevented from doing what you desire to do. But if you are guided (led) by the [Holy] Spirit, you are not subject to the Law (Galatians 5:16-18, AMP).

Out the Window It Goes!

You may as well throw all your will power out the window; it won't help you become more holy. Remember that your best will never be enough! Why do we labor to remain in the flesh and perform to get God to be pleased with us? It's all about mindsets, traditions, and wrong belief systems. Again, *we must change our minds and our focus.* The way to be free from our fleshly desires is not to continue focusing on what we should do, but to focus on what Jesus has already done right! In other words, once again, focusing on our righteousness in Christ empowers us to resist temptation and, thus, overcome. You are seated with Christ in heavenly places. See yourself that way and you will begin to overcome! Read below:

And God raised us up with Christ and seated us
with him in the heavenly realms in Christ Jesus, in
order that in the coming ages he might show the
incomparable riches of his grace, expressed in his
kindness to us in Christ Jesus. For it is by grace you
have been saved, through faith—and this not from
yourselves, it is the gift of God—not by works, so
that no one can boast. For we are God's handiwork,
created in Christ Jesus to do good works, which
God prepared in advance for us to do (Ephesians
2:6-10).

Sons and daughters of God, listen up once more. The
only way we can experience right standing with God is through
Jesus' death and His resurrection. And, as you know by now, we
must accept the price that He paid as a gift. The Word explains
how to accept this gift:

That if thou shalt confess with thy mouth the Lord
Jesus, and shalt believe in thine heart that God hath
raised him from the dead, thou shalt be saved. For
with the heart man believeth unto righteousness;
and with the mouth confession is made unto
salvation. For the scripture saith, Whosoever
believeth on him shall not be ashamed (Romans
10:9-11, KJV).

Of course, faith is involved as we believe in our hearts
that we are justified and when we confess with our mouths that
we are saved. But, we need to receive the simplicity of the truth
that speaking the Lordship of Jesus over our lives and believing
in His resurrection places us in right standing with God.

Amazing, isn't it? So simple—so true—such a reality if we believe and receive this incredible gift.

I'm excited that you have determined to keep reading. And, I am positive that the Holy Spirit has been speaking to your heart and especially that He has been setting you free from every yoke of self-righteousness. Believer, more revelation and freedom await in the following chapters if you just keep reading. First, let's take some time for self-reflection as I believe it will reinforce your relationship with the Lord.

A Time of Reflection

In this time of self-reflection, I believe that it is important to revisit the reasons why you have been performance-driven in order to achieve right standing with God. I'm certain you have highlighted and/or underlined areas in this book that have ministered to your spirit. Maybe you can glance over the dog-eared pages and reflect on all the areas of your heart where the Holy Spirit has ministered truth. Take a few moments to review some of those passages. You've learned a lot in this journey. The Holy Spirit wants to meet with you right now. Pull aside, talk to Him, and listen to Him. Then, answer the questions below:

1. Self-righteousness is our own attempt to be righteous, loved, and accepted. Have you noticed a pattern of self-righteousness and pride in your own life? If so, describe the pattern below.

2. Now, precious believer, look again at what you have written concerning patterns of pride and self righteousness. Take a moment and repent to the Lord for your attempts to be righteous in your own strength.

3. Describe below what you have learned concerning sin consciousness and being God conscious?

4.   Describe times in your life when you did your very best to please God. Explain what striving in the flesh did for you? In other words, were you completely worn out trying to please Him? Do you believe it really accomplished what was intended in your heart?

5.   Describe how to experience the freedom that Christ desires to give.

6.   Explain how to receive this incredible gift of righteousness.

Believer, you are doing great! I know that you are excited to learn that you don't have to be perfect for God to love you. Isn't it freeing to know that you no longer have to perform in order to be holy? And, isn't it wonderful to realize that no matter what we have ever done, God is "never not" pursuing us?

CHAPTER 8

When All Hope Fails

"Hope deferred makes the heart sick, but when the desire is
fulfilled, it is a tree of life" (Proverbs 13:12, AMP).

T here is a type of failure that will lock us down and even
lock us up. It's an imprisonment all on its own. It's
when all hope is gone—it went *kaput*—nothing left
within us to help pick us back up. Hope fails after long periods
of hope deferred. When hopelessness seems to have a
permanent vice-grip on your ability to expect circumstances to
change—when you just can't hold your head up long enough to
give yourself just one more pep talk—or when the timing of a
breakthrough is drawn out so long you feel you are about to
come apart at the seams, *you're experiencing hope deferred*. And,
as you read on, do not despair as I identify the overpowering
feelings of being without hope. Press forward to the solutions I
will give you from God's perspective.

I've been there. I'll bet you've been there also. Hope
deferred. Better yet, we could give it another name: torment!
The problem is that you feel like a failure because it's just not
"supposed" to keep happening to you. It seems to cycle back
like a bad penny. What's so tormenting about hope deferred?
To begin with, it feels as if we've been captured by an

unforeseen enemy. In fact, one of the words used in Scripture to define "deferred hope" is the word "seize." Yep. At some time in your life, hope deferred has attempted to place you under siege and completely lock you down. The result is a gloomy overshadowing sense of failure, and there seems to be nothing you can do about your situation.

Often in our minds and emotions, we connect hope deferred with a sense of personal failure. When needed breakthroughs are prolonged and we lock into believing that *we* have failed in the midst of the trial, we soon believe we are a *total* failure. That's when it's really difficult to get back up. There is a vast difference in failing and being a failure. Hope deferred affects who we are; not what we've done.

Yes, life can knock us down sometimes. The enemy takes advantage during hope deferred. Yes, satan looks for opportunities to deliver "sucker-punches" of hopelessness, despair, and anxiety. He will even attempt to close doors to your breakthroughs, tempting you to distrust God. If satan can get you to bow down to hopelessness and come into agreement with his lies that falsely accuse God, then you will most certainly find yourself in a deep pit! But, read on! There is hope!

Waiting on God

The Hebrew word for "hope" is *towcheleth* (pronounced to-kheh'-leth) which translates as "expectation or to expect with confidence." It is rooted in another Hebrew word, *yachal*, (pronounced yaw-chal') and it means to "wait;" it is implied to mean to be patient. It is also connected to words that express the fact that hope may actually tarry, but to trust and wait. So you see, when hope (trust and the ability to wait) is deferred (drawn out over long periods of time), we will be tempted to waver in our trust in God. After all, He should be coming through with His promises! Then, we will cycle into introspection and blame ourselves for the situations we are facing. We might even believe that God is punishing us for some type of sin and that He is deliberately withholding breakthrough. We touched on this in the previous chapter when I wrote about our need to measure up. When we fall short we blame ourselves and believe the lie that we are a failure in life. Hope deferred does cause us to become more introspective and consistently look for a flaw in our lives rather that boldly and confidently declare who we are in Christ.

Believe me: the devil would love for you to blame God for your problem. It is true that God has His divine timing, and we need to always be on His timetable. And, yes, the enemy can use this to cause us to become bitter toward God. However, to cycle out of deferred hope requires that we eat from the Tree of Life. Proverbs 13:12 reminds us of this fact: the tree of life and fulfilled desires are connected. One fruit from that tree is patience, and another fruit is trust. These are two types of fruit of which we must partake during times that hope is deferred.

Hopelessness and Failure

I can't begin to tell you how many times I have had to encourage members in the Body of Christ concerning hopelessness. It's at epidemic levels across the board. Parents have become filled with despair over their children. Many pastors have believed for a building to serve the community since the beginning of their ministry, and they are still waiting for the breakthrough. Others have struggled financially for years, and it seems hopeless at this point that their congregants and their churches will ever become successful. Business owners need to expand, but they do not have the resources available to do so. It's clear that we seem trapped when we are hopeless, and we feel like failures.

Actual failure is very closely connected to hope deferred and hopelessness. Though you may not have connected the two, let me affirm that hope deferred causes us to believe there is no end to the misery that is experienced. If you are a "fixer" in life or a type of "rescuer," it's even worse for you! In other words, if you can't fix it or rescue someone from their problem, you believe you have failed them (and yourself!).

It's a type of imprisonment similar to being a slave who has no options in life. These situations become similar to a prison cell with a solid steel door and no window. Worse yet, the door is locked, and no one knows who has a key. It's hopeless!

A pit is similarly dark, lonely, and isolated just like a prison cell, right? No one desires to be put in a pit or a prison. Hopelessness coupled with a sense of failure in life will cause a complete lock down to your faith. Let's take some time and talk about this some more.

I know...if you didn't realize you were feeling hopeless or have maybe been feeling that way when you began this chapter, you realize it now! If you are in a pit or feel like you are a slave to hopelessness, *keep reading*. I believe this book is in your hands now so that you can have faith to cycle out of the darkness you are experiencing. You picked up this book because you feel like a failure. You've messed up. You've missed God's timing. Maybe you've made a bad decision, and you need God to turn it all around for the good—NOW!

A Mess Up Isn't Permanent Failure

Precious one, we all have messed up at sometime in life, but that doesn't mean that we are a failure. We've all been tempted to give up on God—maybe we actually did throw the towel in the ring, and quit believing for the breakthrough. Quite possibly we walked out on God. However, He has never, never walked out on us! When life seems hopeless He is still the anchor of our hope (see Hebrews 6:19, ASV)! His anchor reaches the deepest pit and the darkest dungeons that become our prison cells. God will always see to it that we experience an opportunity to see beyond a tear-stained past and regain hope and vision for the future. He promises us that. But, we must continue to remain positioned to eat from the Tree of Life; it's all about making the right choice.

Your pit is no different than the one in which I found myself. Sometimes I find myself back into familiar surroundings and realize that I've been here before! I have had to adjust my "feel sorry for me" attitude many times. There is no life in self-pity; it's definitely fruit from a wrong source. The way to cycle out of self-pity is to remember God's faithfulness during our past experiences and re-connect with Him again through trust. If we do that, we will always have renewed hope for the future! As you walk through this chapter, please know that you are not walking alone. Jesus is holding your hand; the Holy Spirit is leading you into all truth! You will come out of this prison—this pit of darkness and hopelessness!

Unfulfilled Desire

Before we go any further, I want you to understand the evil power behind hope deferred and hopelessness. As I mentioned earlier, hopelessness is often a result of unfulfilled desire. Hopelessness takes a sense of lack on a journey that will rend your soul if you camp out there and decide to surrender to what you are experiencing in the natural. You need *supernatural eyesight* at this time—eyes to see what God has promised for your future.

The enemy will capitalize upon hopelessness to isolate you from those who care about you. Satan desires to separate you from the Body so that you are cut off from your lifeline. The Word instructs us to remain connected to the Body of Christ (see Ephesians 4:16). This is because each of us has something that someone else needs; we all need each other to survive! But, there is more to winning the war against hope deferred and unfulfilled desire. Hopeless is also a result of an *unrenewed mind*. The biggest battle you will fight in spiritual warfare is right between your ears. Our minds must be renewed to understand who we are in Christ.

As I mentioned earlier, it's tempting to become introspective and fault-finding when we do not experience our dreams, hopes, and expectations. Hopelessness is cemented into our minds and hearts when we don't recognize our prayers answered and desires realized. Since hopelessness makes the heart sick, our hearts will become bitter, and we will become negative and narrow-minded. *A belief system like that will position us to focus on our own ability to get out of a slimy pit.* Yet, all the while, only Christ can deliver us. To believe it is up to us, individually, to fix the problem causes us to carry a heavier load without the grace to carry it! And, if we focus on being good enough for God to help us out of that prison cell or pit, our faith will falter. Why is that? Because our faith must be in His ability and not our own!

When we focus on our sins and remain sin conscious, it will weaken us rather than empower us. This type of thinking will keep us cycling in failure and despair. Then, as a result we believe (wrongly, of course) hopelessness deserves a home in us!

Getting Past the Pit of Our Past

The problem with so many of us is that we cannot get past our past. In a way, our past can become a pit or another form of imprisonment. Your pit may have wallpaper that shouts, "You're a complete failure." Maybe your prison wall screams, "You've been married three times. What a failure you are. Your future is hopeless; you'll never experience a successful marriage." Your prison may completely confine you to a dead-end job (or life!) and you feel trapped. Hopelessness creeps in, and before you know it, you are consumed with despair.

The enemy thrives on reminding us of our past failures and sins. He would like nothing more than to keep you in lockdown. I have to admit, it's difficult to get past a sin from our past. Yet, we must renew our mind to the fact that we have been delivered from a sin-nature. Yes, when we become born-again we are born into a new nature. The old man passes away, and we become new. The enemy attempts to keep us chained to the old, dead man. Now, that would definitely be bondage to drag a corpse around all day, wouldn't it? Yet, we do that at times, don't we? Those of us who are believers must understand that we are no longer slaves to an old sin nature. The old sin nature died when we received Jesus as our Lord and Savior. Again, the problem is that our minds need renewing as to who we now are once we have become born-again. If we do not understand that we are no longer slaves to our past nature, we will become sin-conscious. I know I keep hammering this in, but it is necessary to understand that a sin-conscious person will continue to struggle with hope deferred because he/she is looking to self rather than to Jesus and His finished work at the cross.

I believe it is safe to conclude at this point that hope deferred is the same as experiencing a locked door that is impossible to open on our own. Hopelessness can be a pit into which we plunge and can't seem to get out. Often we might even wish to die. This is because when hopelessness overshadows us with its foreboding darkness it will attempt to prophesy more despair. Hope deferred breeds more discontentment, disappointment, and self-introspection; all of these leading us to believe that we are a complete failure in life. Our natural response is to question ourselves, "What did I do wrong to be in this place?" Or, we may think, "I'm a complete failure in life." These are the thoughts that are connected to a hurting heart and sheer hopelessness. But, it is also the result of believing that it is up to us and our doing everything right to please God. Dear believer, we can never be righteous enough to please God or righteous enough for Him to fulfill our dreams and desires. Only because of Jesus and what was accomplished at the cross are we empowered to get out of the pit of despair, renew our minds concerning the goodness of God, and shift into a place where we expect and experience breakthrough!

Hope Deferred, Barrenness, and God's Tests

Hope deferred leaves an imprint of barrenness. Hannah understood it. Her husband Elkanah loved her, even though she had no children by him. Yet, Hannah was completely in despair. I believe she felt like a complete failure because she could not give her husband children. How do you rise up in faith when you believe you have failed? Well, keep reading. Hannah gives us a beneficial clue to cycling out of this type of foreboding failure. Scripture lays it out there for us right up front that Hannah must have felt like a failure in life: "He had two wives; one was called Hannah and the other Peninnah. Peninnah had children, but Hannah had none" (1 Samuel 1:2).

Did you get that? Elkanah's other wife had children; Hannah had none. She felt cursed with barrenness. Barrenness is similar to a disease which eats away at hope, day after day after day. As with hope deferred, one might wish to die without a breakthrough. Many in Scripture had wished to die. Elijah was one of those. We've already studied about his life in chapter five. He ran to the wilderness after receiving a death threat from Jezebel, "But he went a day's journey into the wilderness and came and sat down under a lone broom or juniper tree and asked that he might die. He said, 'It is enough; now, O Lord, take away my life; for I am no better than my fathers'" (1 Kings 19:4, AMP). Realizing he was no better than his fathers before him caused him to sink into great despair. We discussed how the pride of Elijah was beginning to unravel at this point. A wilderness will do that to us; it forces us to recognize our weakness and our dependence upon God. Though Elijah was still running from God, the Lord in His goodness and mercy sent an angel to care for him to ensure that he reached his destiny. Would God do less for us? Absolutely not. Remember: He is *"never not"* pursuing you!

Rachel told her husband Jacob to give her children or she would die (see Genesis 30:1). To me, this reads as if she would rather be dead than barren. Remember, there is no hope in barrenness. Yet, Scripture says that God remembered Rachel and gave her children. For more on Rebecca, I encourage you to read my recent book, *Silencing the Accuser: Eight Lies Satan Uses Against Believers* (Chosen Books, 2011), which discusses God's covenant with her and us today.

Jonah prayed to die when he surrendered to God's plans and went to Nineveh (see Jonah 4:3). He could have died in the belly of the whale, but God had a plan for Jonah; He just waited for Jonah to wave the white flag! But, Jonah was not barren; he was outright self-centered. He doesn't fit in the category of hope deferred except maybe that his pride made him a hopeless case for God to use any further. I'm convinced of that God loved Jonah; however, God's love is meant to empower us to be instruments of His glory. Jonah wanted his own glory—a glorious reputation. Being used for His glory is not limited to our always experiencing a sun-shiny day after day after day. Though we are promised God's blessings, none of us escapes tests that are given by Him. Sometimes His tests are in a wilderness of hopelessness which are meant to cause us to honor His presence and rise up to praise Him even when we don't feel like it.

It's true that God's love is never-ending, and we have a never-ending destiny in Him if we receive His love and submit to His plans for our lives. Jonah was bitter because God had His own plans for an entire city, not limited to a single prophet. Jonah's mission ends with Nineveh. Sadly, his history is completed after only four chapters!

If you read Psalm 7, you will notice that David also prayed to die (see v. 5). No, it wasn't written after his sin of adultery and murder, but he desired to die because of false accusations from King Saul. David despaired and even wished to die. However, as I mentioned in an earlier chapter, David knew how to cycle out of despair by focusing on God's love for him. Good for David! What an awesome legacy for us to follow. I have realized that when I am falsely accused, God will use it as a test. Will I believe what God says about me or what man says? Passing the test involves understanding my identity in Christ. An identity crisis often occurs during times when hope is deferred. David understood who he was in the eyes of His Lord. Do we? If we can see ourselves as God sees us, we will become more empowered to cycle out of despair.

Peter told Jesus he would die with Him (see Matthew 26:35). But, we all know that Peter's zeal led to some serious rebukes from Jesus (see Matthew 14:31). He seemed to say all the right words at the wrong time. However, Scripture states that *all* the disciples agreed with Peter that they would die with Him. Without Jesus remaining with them on earth, I'm sure their future seemed hopeless. However, after Jesus' resurrection, it is noted that many went on instructed by Christ to do even greater things. We will discuss Peter a little later, but for now know that he and the disciples are counted among those who at one time asked for God to allow them to die.

> **AN IDENTITY CRISIS OFTEN OCCURS DURING TIMES WHEN HOPE IS DEFERRED.**

Hannah's Desire to Live

Hannah may have decided, as did Rachel, that if God didn't give her children she would be better off dead, but we don't read that she said that. We do notice, however, that she rose up in her faith and took a firm stand. Keep reading; this passage will definitely encourage you and build your faith for a breakthrough.

Scripture notes that year after year Hannah was reminded of her barrenness. She would cycle into despair and hopelessness—neither eating nor drinking. I'm sure she fought back the temptation to believe that she was a complete failure. Weeping for days on end, her husband attempted to comfort her. Then one day "when they had finished eating and drinking in Shiloh, Hannah stood up" (1 Samuel 1:9a). Sometimes when we are in a cycle of hope deferred we need to take a stand against it! Hannah decided to do something about it; she took a stand by visiting the temple to pray to God. The word "stood up" is connected to the words referring to our *making a decree*. Hannah went to the temple and made a vow or made a declaration (decree) that if God would give her a son, she would give the son back to Him.

Hannah was so out of control with her weeping that she appeared intoxicated to the priest, Eli. She explained that she was not drinking, but was praying out of anguish. Eli blessed her and sent her away with the promise that God would answer her prayers. Hannah left the temple with restored hope and renewed vision. In the course of time, she became pregnant and gave birth to a son, Samuel—one of God's greatest prophets.

Again, Hannah never prayed to die. In fact, I believe that her hope to have a child kept her alive. I love that about her; even though nothing appeared to be happening on her behalf, she kept on living. But one day she "stood up!" Her faith rose up and she was empowered, even in the midst of weeping, to make a godly decree. Maybe it's time for us to decree what is in our hearts.

God is NOT Punishing You!

Since we equate prison with punishment, our default button during difficult times is to believe that we have done something to offend or upset God. If we are the type who believes we fail to measure up in life, then we are expecting punishment. Hope deferred is punishment; some of us believe we even deserve it!

As we're in that pit, fear creeps into our hearts. We fear that there is no way out! Allow me to encourage you at this point. Jesus Christ came to set the prisoners free! He is the one who opens the prison doors! In fact, He promises to help you take a firm stand in faith during the midst of adversity and hopelessness. Read what David said (and if anyone should know about the goodness of God in the midst of despair, it would be him!):

> He lifted me out of the slimy pit, out of the mud
> and mire; he set my feet on a rock and gave me a
> firm place to stand. He put a new song in my
> mouth, a hymn of praise to our God. Many will see
> and fear and put their trust in him (Psalm 40:2-3).

I wanted to include both verses of this passage up front. Psalm 40:2 addresses the immediate need to have hope for getting out of the pit. It is clear that it is He that lifts us out of the slimy pit and empowers us to stand. However, it is clear in verse 3 that there is a faith step required for us. That faith step is to "sing praises" and to "trust" God. We will address the faith step in a bit as we gain knowledge of the importance of taking a firm stand and making godly decrees.

For now, let's focus on God lifting us out of the pit which is so often connected to a lack of hope, a deferred hope, wavering faith, and consuming unbelief.

Decreeing the Desire

If you recall the original purpose of this chapter was to expose and defeat hope deferred. Since we often believe we have failed in life during times of deferred hope, I felt it necessary to write about this subject. The discussion along the way to victory over hopelessness and despair (and feelings of failure) is connected directly to getting to the place where we recognize the fruition of the desire of our hearts. Let's look again at Proverbs 13:12: "Hope deferred makes the heart sick, but when the desire is fulfilled, it is a tree of life" (AMP).

It is clear by this passage that in order to experience the fullness of life we need to experience the desires of our hearts. When I was a young girl I had many different dreams concerning my life. I dreamed of a great marriage—which I have. I dreamed of having a wonderful job—which I also have. I dreamed of having children—which I have a beautiful, wonderful daughter. However, are the dreams exactly as I pictured? To some degree, yes; to some degree, no. Life has taken different turns and, as a result, choices and decisions are made that help shape our future. The key is not to get stuck while you're dreaming. In other words, don't limit God just keep dreaming.

I have heard it said that God wants to give us our hearts' desires, and He will change our desires to become His desires. This is true, but it's not a given. I don't sit around and worry about my dreams; I just keep dreaming. I leave the perfecting up to Him. I firmly believe that God wants us to dream—and dream again. Dreaming with God is limitless living! No need to worry if your dreams are from God; He knows how to perfect them along life's journeys.

Hope deferred steals our ability to dream. In this chapter, I have given keys and steps to empower you to eat from the Tree of Life and cycle out of hope deferred and a sense of failure. Have faith—keep moving forward and keep dreaming!

Making Decrees

There is a connection to making decrees and recognizing the desires of your heart. Let's observe what Job said, "You shall also decide and decree a thing, and it shall be established for you; and the light [of God's favor] shall shine upon your ways" (Job 22:28, AMP).

Job gives us hope in his own hopelessness. Who else lost as much as Job? Yet, he persevered and loved God. In my book, *Silencing the Accuser: Eight Lies Satan Uses Against Believers* (Chosen, 2011), I write an entire chapter about Job, his "false" comforters, and his ability to trust God in the midst of incredible despair. Though my intent is not to write much more on Job, I would like to insert a portion of the chapter that I believe will encourage you. Notice that Job learned through hope deferred to shift into a heartfelt worship unto God. This is a key to us who have experienced failure to any degree:

> The book's champion, Job (*Iyyob* in Hebrew), is an example of a righteous man who walked in integrity and eventually endured tremendous suffering but

never blamed God. Though he had many questions and many times asked God why, Job submitted to his Lord's faithfulness. More than thirty chapters are devoted to Job's searching his soul. Attempting to find a reason for his misfortune, he debated his friends, who were influenced by the Accuser. Yet after the exhausting and tragic encounters, Job no longer cared why because his heart had melted into continual worship (page 23).

It was Job who gave us a heads up concerning the decree. He said once you decide, make a decree. Then he states that after the decree is made, "It shall be established for you." We will stop here for a bit and re-examine the first portion of this passage. In the beginning of this chapter, I referred to renewing the mind. When we eat from the Tree of Life (feasting on the Words of Jesus Christ), we are renewing our minds to God's truths. Making godly decrees that will cycle you out of despair and hopelessness; it is one of the ways in which your mind becomes renewed. You will notice that the book of Job points out some necessary steps for us to take:

Step One: Decide. Before we make a decree, there is a time to "stand up" just as Hannah did. When we decide on something, something on the inside stands up!

Years ago I was told of a disobedient child who was being disciplined by his father. As his punishment, the father gave specific instructions to sit in the corner. When the father asked his son if he understood why he was being punished, he replied, "Yes, I'm sitting down on the outside, but I am standing up on the inside!" Well, that is what I feel whenever the enemy is attempting to cause me to believe something opposite of what God has stated concerning me, my identity, or my future. I may cower down at first, but there is never a change until I finally take a firm stand against the spirit of hopelessness and despair. Many times hopelessness is connected to the accuser of the brethren. (I have written in great detail how the accuser of the brethren targets our lives and destinies).

To be even more specific, the accuser will attempt to mark us with failure through guilt and shame. *Guilt and shame* are so closely connected to failure that it is difficult to write about them separately. For now, know that barrenness will result in extreme grief and even premature death if we don't take a firm stand against the lies that are connected to it. The lies of the enemy which are connected to this are:

- "You will never bear fruit. You are marked with barrenness and failure."
- "You will never see your dreams fulfilled."
- "Because you are a worthless sinner, God will not answer your prayers."
- "Your sin has separated you from God's love."
- "You cannot be blessed. You are doomed for failure."
- "Look at your life. You are a failure at all that you attempt to accomplish."
- "You don't measure up."
- "You are flawed and unworthy of God's love."

Dear one, I am reminded of the encouragement given to us by the apostle Paul: "Stand therefore [hold your ground], having tightened the belt of truth around your loins and having put on the breastplate of integrity and of moral rectitude and right standing with God" (Ephesians 6:14, AMP).

Did you notice that when you stand, you also "hold your ground?" Yes, God has given you ground to protect. That ground is your identity in Christ. That same ground involves your destiny and being further used as an instrument for His glory. You have an inheritance as a son/daughter in Christ. Hold on to it and don't allow the enemy to steal it from you by believing his lies concerning you! Keep your belt of truth on; don't take it off! I have had people in church ask me; "Pastor Sandie, did you put on your armor today?" My response is, "I don't ever take it off!" What has caused us to think that we take it off at night when we sleep? We need the armor 24/7!

Another part of this passage deserves mentioning again. Notice that we are to "stand (in our) right standing with God." Precious believer, nothing—absolutely nothing—can take away your righteousness. Righteousness means "right standing." You are righteous because of the blood of Jesus and the finished work at the cross. You are not righteous because of your religion, your religious works, your own holiness, your doctrine, or your belief system. You are only righteous because Christ is righteous. Because of that, you cannot lose your righteousness! Take a firm stand in that, connect your faith with that truth, and then you are empowered to shift into your destiny!

Step Two: Make a decree. A decree is a written declaration. However, it can also be a verbal declaration into the airways that will defeat the enemy. Esther made one, and she saved an entire nation. When we study her life, we recognize how this orphaned Jewish girl had to endure much preparation before she was empowered to hold her ground against an enemy fueled by satan himself, Haman. Haman was an Amalekite, (an ancient enemy of the Jews), who sought to destroy the entire Jewish race. Satan worked through Haman to falsely accuse Esther's beloved uncle Mordecai and the Jews, even to the point of convincing King Artaxerxes to destroy all the Jews in Persia. Esther had to rise above any possible rejection, abandonment issues, fear, betrayal, and false accusations. And, eventually, she was positioned in a level of governmental authority to reverse death decrees against herself and her people; even influencing the king to issue a decree that would restore the Jewish nation once again to prominence. Take a moment and grab your prayer journal. Or, use the margins on this page to write a decree that comes to your mind. Write what God says about you; it will negate every false accusation that the enemy has declared!

Step Three: Have faith that it is established! Once a stand is made and the decree is written, then take a moment and settle it in your spirit that it is established! It is done. Know in your heart that because of the finished work at the cross, your victory was established. No devil, no ungodly decree, and no wicked plan from satan can remove you from your right standing in Christ. You are righteous. You are loved. You are a success, and you are blessed. According to God's Word over your life, He has promised you His best. You are royalty—a child of the King. Even if you have failed in life, rest assured that His promise over you and your life is never negated by a circumstance.

Step Four: Enter into divine favor. If you recall, we discussed God's grace earlier. Grace is not limited to unmerited favor, but it also encompasses a supernatural ability and empowerment to fulfill destiny. Grace is God's power given to us to remain obedient. We cannot remain obedient in our own strength; the strength to fulfill destiny comes from grace.

To sum it all up: First, we take a stand against hopelessness and the seductions of the enemy who lies and says that you are a hopeless failure. Secondly, we write or speak a decree that negates every negative decree of the enemy. Remember, decrees can also be spoken. Quoting God's Word and His promises concerning your life is a great weapon against the enemy. Either one, a written or spoken decree, is effective in your spiritual warfare against hope deferred and a sense of ongoing failure and despair. Next, we lock into faith that it is done—it is established—due to the cross. Now, let your faith arise as you take off the old garments of shame and guilt and put on new garments of praise! You are entering into divine favor!

A Time of Reflection

1.   If you have ever felt as if you were in a pit, this chapter was definitely meant for you to read. Take a moment and describe your pit. Look closely at your pit. Is there "wallpaper" on the walls of your pit? If so, what is written on the wall of your pit? Maybe you notice words like: "You are hopeless," "Your life is a failure," or "You will never achieve success in life." Write below, in your own words, whatever your wallpaper states about you:

2.   Hope deferred is sometimes defined as "seized." Do you relate to happiness, hope, and fruitfulness being under "siege?" Is the accuser of the brethren attempting to keep you seized in a hopeless prison through his false accusations? If you answered "yes" to either question, describe your siege or seizure below:

3. Now it is time to write, once more, what the Lord says about you. It is your opportunity to write a decree! In this chapter you read how to rise up, take a firm stand, and make a decree. Write below your godly decrees that reverse the words written on your pit's wallpaper and also reverse your seizure experiences. Just as Queen Esther reversed a death decree, you can reverse any area of unfruitfulness with your divine decree.

4. I, _____(insert your name), on this date being _____, write this divine decree.

5. Now, believer, acknowledge that you have divine favor!

CHAPTER 9

The Power of Revelation

T his chapter might possibly be the most powerful chapter you will read on this journey. Though you have read most of the way through to the end, I purposefully chose to place this chapter at the book's conclusion. Up until now, you have read about several challenges we face when attempting to overcome any type of failure. You've read about God's desire for us to be successful in life, how He gives us grace to fulfill our earthly assignment, and how to have a new mind set concerning His goodness.

You have been encouraged by reading about different biblical characters that faced failures, yet were able to regain faith and momentum in life. Yes, you have been learning how to think as a champion by understanding and confessing who you are in God. You have been empowered to live a righteous-conscious life rather than a sin-conscious life that would restrain you from limitless living. And, you have read how to focus on what Jesus has done right—not what you've done wrong because your very best is never good enough! Now, in this chapter, we will look at the life of Peter and how he received a revelation concerning the deity of Christ. Though he later failed in his loyalty during a test, the revelation he had previously received became the rudder that guided his ship throughout the rest of his life. Dear believer, revelation will be your rudder in life to navigate you through storms and be a main contributor to fulfilling your God-given dreams and divine destiny.

Revealing What is Hidden

The word *revelation* means "to reveal something that is hidden or to disclose what was once unknown and make it known." As you know, Jesus taught with parables that were stories that contained what He referred to as "secrets and mysteries." Let's observe what Jesus said concerning these secrets and mysteries:

> Then the disciples came to Him and said, Why do You speak to them in parables? And He replied to them, To you it has been given to know the secrets and mysteries of the kingdom of heaven, but to them it has not been given. For whoever has [spiritual knowledge], to him will more be given and he will be furnished richly so that he will have abundance; but from him who has not, even what he has will be taken away. This is the reason that I speak to them in parables: because having the power of seeing, they do not see; and having the power of hearing, they do not hear, nor do they grasp and understand (Matthew 13:10-13, AMP).

Let's talk about the previous passage. Jesus knew that the religious people could both see and hear in the natural, but were completely blocked spiritually because they refused to receive the truths concerning the kingdom of God. Therefore, Jesus would pull aside and reveal to the disciples the hidden truths within the parables; these stories contained secrets that had been hidden, but were not being revealed to the masses.

> **GOD HIDES TRUTH—NOT FROM US, BUT FOR US!**

To access heaven and bring the will of heaven to earth, we must know God's thoughts and be able to see what has yet been unseen. This is where the need for revelation comes into play. Many truths have been hidden, but God's heart is to have a seeing and hearing people to receive these truths. It's important to understand this: God hides truth—not from us, but for us! It's important to understand this because during times of uncertainty, we often default to a "God is mad at me" false belief system. When revelation is hidden, His desire is that we seek Him for the answers we need—the revelation needed for our shift!

Being Cut Off from Fulfilling Destiny

Without revelation we will perish which means that we will be controlled by hopelessness and despair. We are instructed by God to choose life or death—there's no in-between. Therefore, knowing that Hosea 4:6 says, "My people are destroyed for a lack of knowledge" and Isaiah 5:13 states that "my people go into exile for their lack of knowledge," it's easy to conclude that we need knowledge—especially knowledge contained within hidden mysteries!

Reader, listen up. We are "destroyed" when we don't have godly knowledge. The word "destroyed" means *cease and completely cut off*. When we don't have revelation, we will become cut off from the voice of God, His direction, and His blessings. Therefore, we will "go into exile." This means we will go into captivity and be completely stripped of all we have—

being completely disgraced. Now, I'm not talking about losing your salvation; I am referring to us being cut-off from all that heaven has to offer!

Dear one, my heart is not to frighten you with condemnation. No! What I purpose to do is to relate to you the importance of revelation. Without pressing into God through an intimate relationship and not religious works, the enemy can easily move right into our lives, homes, churches, businesses, families, etc. and strip us, humiliate us, and set us up for continual failure.

However, when we receive revelation, faith always arises. How is that? Well, precious believer, God says that when we call out to Him, He answers us and will "show thee great and mighty things, which thou knowest not" (Jeremiah 33:3, KJV). You see, God desires to reveal what is unknown. Remember, revelation is hidden for us and not from us. If you have a problem and you continually fail, rest in God for He has answers that will empower you to live a fruitful life of abundance!

Revelation releases fresh vision for your future. Proverbs 29:18 reminds us, "Where there is no revelation, the people cast off restraint" (NKJV). The King James Version states it differently as it says, "Where there is no vision, the people perish." For years I believed that these verses were speaking about having goals and dreams that bring personal fulfillment. However, it's really about having the same vision that God does. We need to see what He sees in us! Whatever God dreams for us, we see them and connect with heaven so that they are fulfilled. His revelation concerning us and all that concerns us becomes our revelation. There is no failure that can withstand God's revelation for our lives. He is a BIG God, and He thinks BIG about us!

Peter's Revelation

One familiar incident in the New Testament where revelation was revealed to mankind is in Matthew 16:13-19. Take a few moments to read through this short passage and see if you notice what the revelation was and how revelation was described by Jesus:

> Now when Jesus came into the parts of Caesarea Philippi, he asked his disciples, saying, Who do men say that the Son of man is? And they said, Some say John the Baptist; some, Elijah; and others, Jeremiah, or one of the prophets. He saith unto them, But who say ye that I am? And Simon Peter answered and said, Thou art the Christ, the Son of the living God. And Jesus answered and said unto him, Blessed art thou, Simon Bar-Jonah: for flesh and blood hath not revealed it unto thee, but my Father who is in heaven. And I also say unto thee, that thou art Peter, and upon this rock I will build my church; and the gates of Hades shall not prevail against it. I will give unto thee the keys of the kingdom of heaven: and whatsoever thou shalt bind on earth shall be bound in heaven; and whatsoever thou shalt loose on earth shall be loosed in heaven (ASV).

Did you notice that Peter was the one who received the revelation that Christ was the Son of the living God? The other disciples did not receive it. How do we know it was a revelation? Because Jesus said that Peter was blessed because flesh and blood had not revealed it...but by His Father who is in heaven. Peter received a download from heaven. And, that particular revelation became the rock upon which Jesus built His church. I know there is a corporate church, but believer, *we, as individuals,* are His church! We are His temple. Therefore, when we receive revelation, that revelation can also become a rock upon which God can build! And the gates of hell will not be able to stand against the power we have because God has given us the keys of the kingdom of Heaven. What are those keys? I'm so glad you asked. The keys of the Kingdom are the power to see into heaven, access what is there, and bring it to earth. Also, if it's not in heaven, it doesn't belong on earth. Sickness is not in heaven; therefore, we bind it up from being on earth.

Continuing with Peter

So Peter got a brownie point that day with Jesus. Wow! I can just imagine Peter thinking, *Jesus called me a rock, and He is building the church upon what I said. Hmmm...*Wonder what else I can say that could get me more attention?

Peter seemed to be the disciple who had the right things to say, but so often at the wrong times. In the previous case, he accessed heaven—saw and heard—and received revelation. Other times...well, he, as well as others, may conclude that he failed to a degree. Poor Peter. He didn't understand that revelation is not given to make us appear smarter or more intelligent. We could all learn a lesson from him: when we find success, don't act astonished or be impressed with self! Revelation is intended to bring forth transformation. Transformation involves change, but it also creates atmospheres of enlargement. God wanted to enlarge the thinking of his disciples, but also His kingdom. This results in our receiving and walking in our God-given inheritance.

Peter's Challenges

Let's observe some of Peter's challenges—he might describe them as disappointments? After all, most of us have been disappointed in ourselves from time to time, right? Peter was made from a mold that I believe is admirable even though his zeal and passion sometimes got in the way. Like the time Jesus was explaining to his disciples that he would be taken away and that he would suffer and die. Peter took Jesus aside to privately talk to him and began to reprove him. Now, reader, please go with me a bit on this. Can you imagine Peter taking Jesus aside...presumptuously ...believing he could correct Him and set Him straight? Peter counseled Jesus and said, *"No, that's not going to happen!"* I'm thinking, *"Peter, just because you got the answer right the first time doesn't mean you have all the answers!"* But, Jesus went farther than that and actually called Peter "satan!" Read the account below:

> Then Peter took Him aside to speak to Him privately and began to reprove and charge Him sharply, saying, God forbid, Lord! This must never happen to You! But Jesus turned away from Peter and said to him, Get behind Me, Satan! You are in My way [an offense and a hindrance and a snare to Me]; for you are minding what partakes not of the nature and quality of God, but of men (Matthew 16:22-23, AMP).

Reader, please understand that this happened right after Peter had received heaven's revelation of who Jesus was.

Now, in this instance, Peter is wrong; he did not hear from heaven. In fact, Jesus rebuked Him and said he was a hindrance. I have often wondered how Peter responded to that rebuke. He was no longer referred to as a rock, but now satan. Ouch. Big band-aid for this one. Glad it happened to Peter and not me.

Still Being Taught

Right after the rebuke, Jesus instructed all the disciples concerning denying self, denying selfish interests, and focusing on our assignments to promote God's Kingdom (see Matthew 16:24-26). Again, can you imagine Peter's face when Jesus turned from him, gathered all the disciples together, and taught them on the dangers of pride, self-centeredness, and selfish motives? And how the Kingdom mission is greater than personal recognition? (Go ahead; bring the whole box of Band-aids®!). Peter is perplexed: he's right, but now he's wrong. He might be thinking, *"And now he's telling all of the others about me and my blockhead attitude. Now they all know I said something that led to this teaching."*

I remember when I was in elementary school, and I walked up to tell my teacher that the girl who sat behind me was pulling on my pony tail. I didn't like her at all. She was beautiful and had the loveliest hair. She was decked out every day with hair braids, ribbons, shiny shoes, adorable clothes, and yes...to top it off...a handbag for every outfit. Anyway, she barely tugged at my hair because her pencil got caught in my dangling hair ribbon. I knew all the while she didn't mean to irritate me by pulling on my hair, but it seemed a legitimate excuse to complain about her. So, I marched my little self up to the teacher and told her that the girl who sat behind me was pulling on my hair and tearing out my ribbons. And, if she didn't do something about it, I would tell my parents, and they would see to it that the teacher was dealt with. (Oh, man!) The teacher kindly told me she would talk to the girl.

So, I marched my little self back to my desk, gave the girl behind me a shrugged shoulder and arched eyebrow and sat down. Next thing I know, the teacher is telling the entire class to pull out their Bibles because we were going to read about love and how important it was to love one another as we love ourselves.

I felt like sliding under the desk in front of me. I just knew everyone in the room knew she was talking about me and my ridiculous attitude. I felt like an idiot. I was ashamed of myself. I felt like a failure. Maybe Peter felt the same.

Growing and Gaining Knowledge

Success begins at the exact time that we realize that our walk with God is all about "growing" and "gaining knowledge." As we grow in God, we continue to gain knowledge. That's what it's all about! Growing in Him involves acquiring all the necessary knowledge we need to experience *sozo*—the fullness of life.

Peter was on a learning curve. One time he has the right answer. Then it's like we need to say, *"Peter...just go to the end of the line!"* I've been at that place, and it wasn't just in elementary school. I don't like the back of lines; however, sometimes that is our ladder to success. The poet John Keats wrote, "Failure is, in a sense, the highway to success, inasmuch as every discovery of what is false leads us to seek earnestly after what is true." I agree. *Failure doesn't have to remain failure.* Instead, it can be a highway to motivate us to seek what is really true in life. And, what is true is what God says. You are not a failure. You will be empowered for your future by gaining knowledge and understanding the hidden truths regarding the undiscovered greatness God has planned for you!

Think about Peter in Matthew 14:29 where he walked on water! Wow! For a few seconds, his faith was at summit level. Yet, when he focused on the storm, he began to sink. Jesus' response was, "You of little faith, why did you doubt?"

Just like most of us, our faith in God's ability to sustain us or empower us with the supernatural is growing. Peter's faith was in an incubator state—having to be carefully watched and guarded like a premature baby. We don't know how he felt about his sinking "demonstration." Maybe he'd wished he had just stayed in the boat like the others. Maybe he thought he looked ridiculously foolish! But, at least he tried! Go, Peter!

How about when Peter denied Christ three times? How appalling was that? Surely none of us would deny someone we loved—or would we? Have we? And, if we did, we failed that person by not defending them when they were being falsely accused. Or, we didn't correct the illegitimate hearsay, but either joined in or remained silent. Yep, we can all relate to Peter.

Jesus Loved Peter and He Loves Us!

I have often wondered how Peter was able to keep running his race. He failed, or so it appeared, numerous times while being discipled. And, as you were just reminded, at the

186

time of Jesus' greatest need for support, Peter denied ever knowing him. Yet, Jesus still loved Peter—even when betrayal became a reality.

One thing I love about our Savior is that He loves us even when we don't know how to love back. In fact, God has been the One who pursued us, and when we finally saw the Light, we surrendered! It has never been about our finally finding God and how grateful God should be that we are now on His team! No. Even before the foundations of the world Jesus committed to carrying our sins to the cross and giving us eternal life.

I love the fact that even after Jesus died and was resurrected, He had an angel make mention of that one certain disciple, Peter. If you recall, after His death and burial, Mary Magdalene and the other Mary went to his tomb. But, the tomb was empty. Yet, there was an angel who instructed them that He had risen, and they should go and tell His disciples *and tell Peter* to meet Him in Galilee.

Jesus made sure that Peter knew that he would be welcomed by Him. The angel had purposefully singled Peter out from the other disciples. Jesus knew that Peter needed special attention. What a marvelous, forgiving, and understanding Savior we have!

Peter was there, along with the other disciples, when Jesus appeared to the disciples on the after His resurrection. Thomas was there, also. If you recall Thomas is best known as "Doubting Thomas." This is because his faith at one time failed him when he doubted the resurrection. However, he pressed through all doubt, saw Jesus with the other disciples, and ended his mission well. He not only saw Jesus with the others that night, but went on to preach the gospel even as far as India!

Though Peter seemed to always have his foot in his mouth, we can certainly give him credit for leaving all he knew as a fisherman and following Christ. Sure, he was bold-even to his detriment—but, his boldness returned after Jesus died. He was the first to preach after Pentecost when the Holy Spirit came, and the first to preach to the Gentiles. He was also one of the three disciples at Jesus' transfiguration. Peter, though once probably appearing as a square peg pushing its way through a round hole, finished strong. Being transformed from an arrogant and sometimes brash man, he finished in humility.

I think back to when he first received the revelation of who Jesus was. I believe it was revelation that kept this fiery, prideful, once self-sufficient fisherman on track with His true source. Revelation will do that for us. Revelation lifts a veil to allow us to see the light. Revelation empowers each of us to see Him as He is.

Lifting the Veil

Revelation also means "to lift the veil." It means that what once covered you is being removed. Revelation doesn't have a creative quality; it reveals what has always been there. This means that what God says about you is truth, and that particular truth has always been there. Point is that you're just now discovering it!

Even now, God is lifting the veil from your eyes so that you can see truth. Revelation involves seeing truth. You now understand that truth has been hidden us. We've believed a lie for so long. We've believed that we failed and there is no hope. Now, you know the truth about yourself and about God! He has lifted the veil—released revelation. Now you see yourself as God sees you! Nothing is hopeless. Everything can change—especially with revelation. If you remind yourself of who you are in Christ, you will begin to see yourself differently!

In Conclusion

I want to end this book with your receiving the revelation once more concerning what Christ did for you and me. Be encouraged. You have made a lot of progress as you have been on this journey with me. Look at it like this: the mere fact that you are reading this ending chapter betrays every thought the enemy might have to keep you in lock down! You never intended to end up in a pit of hopelessness; however, satan never thought you'd end up at this place of freedom, either!

Precious child of the King, He died for my shame, and He died for your shame. He died for me; He died for you. Dear ones, we are no longer thinking of ourselves as failures. He died for our failure so that we can experience success and blessings. When Jesus took upon Himself our sin, He also took all of our shame of the past. Every failure, disappointment, grief, loss and feeling of lack was nailed to the cross at Calvary.

Let me remind you that God is with you. You already have everything needed to fulfill your purpose in life. Revelation you receive along the way will give necessary knowledge and empower you to access heaven's blessings and breakthroughs.

You are a new creature in Christ. No longer sin-conscious or failure-conscious, but righteous! Now, precious believer, put your faith in God. He promises to watch over every promise and to ensure that you experience them. He is faithful. He loves you. You can have faith in that statement: He loves you. And, because He loves you, He will always see to it that you have the faith you need for every challenge ahead. Yes, you are growing in God. Each bump in the road doesn't disable—it enables! Let your faith arise! There is no need to fear. His perfect love for you will drive every fear away. Fear will no longer steal your faith. You are a champion in God. Run your race. Win the prize. Go for it!

A Time of Reflection

1.   Revelation occurs whenever God makes the "hidden" things or "mysteries" known to His people. Whenever God lifts the veil of the unknown and makes it known to His people, it is called revelation. However, the truth concerning what is revealed has always been there. Is there something you need to hear from God? Do you need revelation today? If so, write your prayer request below. Ask the Lord to empower you to access your Promised Land—your spiritual inheritance—as His child.

2. Ask the Lord to speak to you in the night season. God often speaks through dreams and visions. Before you go to sleep, ask God to speak to you during the night. Your spirit never sleeps so this is a perfect time for Him to speak to you. The Song of Solomon relates a powerful way to fall asleep and hear God where it says, "I sleep, but my heart is awake," (Song of Solomon 5:2a, NKJV). God will visit you in the night season and speak His truths to your heart. This is revelation: His will for your life revealed! Whenever He gives you a dream, ask Him also for the understanding. As dreams come, document at least one of them below along with the understanding of the dream. For more understanding of how to interpret and document your dreams I recommend reading my book *Dream On, Unlocking Your Dreams and Visions* (Zion Ministries, 6th edition, 2011).

About the Author

Dr. Sandie Freed is an internationally recognized speaker and author of over twelve books. Her passion is to empower others to experience freedom in Christ and to impart life transformation to God's people. Sandie always speaks from her heart and her revelation and transparency will captivate your heart to shift into divine purpose. She releases a powerful anointing of healing and hope to those who have been held captive. With a strong anointing of discerning of spirits, Sandie has been known to discern territorial strongholds and release churches and regions from spiritual assignments that withhold finances, deliverances, and breakthroughs. She is also known for her "cutting-edge" prophetic ministry, but also moves very strongly in word of knowledge and miracles.

As a modern day Joseph in dream interpretation, she has become particularly anointed in releasing and activating dreams and visions as well as being strongly gifted with the interpretation. She has hosted and has ministered in numerous Dreams and Visions seminars, whereby she teaches and trains others to interpret dreams. Sandie has been featured numerous times on various radio broadcasts as well as Daystar's "Celebration" program and "Life Today" with James Robinson. In addition to interviews regarding Dreams and Visions, other topics about which Sandie speaks include Overcoming Eating Disorders and Generational Strongholds. Her powerful testimony has ministered to thousands world-wide.

Sandie has traveled nationally and internationally teaching on spiritual discernment. Her ability to accurately prophesy and discern spiritual strongholds over regions has released numerous breakthroughs for individuals and ministries.

Dr. Sandie and Apostle/Pastor Mickey are ordained with Christian International Ministries, serving on their Board of Governors. Sandie presently co-pastors with her husband, Mickey, at Lifegate Church International in Hurst, Texas. They have been married since 1973, and have one daughter, Kimberly; a son-in-law, Daniel Wheeler; and two wonderful grandchildren Elijah and Perrin Wheeler.

Sandie Freed

Author & Speaker

www.SandieFreed.com

Sandie Freed Books

Faith After Failure: Reconnecting with Your Destiny

Failure. It knocks at the doors of our lives and hopes to find permanent residence. The haunting words regarding past failures and doubts resound over and over in our minds until we come to the realization that in God there is no failure! Every obstacle in life is an opportunity for our faith to be renewed and witness the miracle of God's transforming power. God doesn't expect perfection; in fact, He seeks to prove His love and faithfulness by perfecting us as we walk through the challenges of life. This book is all about the times we find ourselves in the pit of despair and are then equipped by God's grace to move forward once again and experience complete fulfillment in Christ. There is no mission impossible for God.

ISBN: 978-1602730557   Parsons Publishing House

Dream On: Unlocking Your Dreams & Visions

Dr. Sandie Freed travels all over the world hosting and teaching in conferences on dreams and visions. Her unique insight has ministered life to people in all walks of life and in all generations. In this book, you can discover how God speaks to us through dreams and visions in a language that is specific to these powerful methods. You will be taught the language of dreams and learn how to interpret various kinds of supernatural communications. Wrapped in this subject, Sandie shares her testimony of deliverance from eating disorders through the use of dreams. Also, find out how to discern counterfeit anointings and false dreams. In this book, you will experience deliverance and freedom through dreams and visions. 6th Edition.

ISBN: 978-0939868490   Zion Ministries

Power in the Blood: Claiming Your Spiritual Inheritance

Spiritual Warfare Expert Helps Believers Claim Their Spiritual Inheritance. What Christians often forget is that they are royalty—children of the one true King. They are royalty not through works but through Jesus' blood, the blood that bought them, that saved them. And in his blood is their inheritance: eternal life, authority, destiny, wisdom, and more! With a discerning perspective gained from years in spiritual warfare and prophetic ministry, Sandie Freed offers life-transforming advice on how believers can rediscover their spiritual ancestry, awaken to their royal identities, and claim the inheritance God is holding for them.

ISBN: 978-0800795511   Chosen Books

Sandie Freed Books

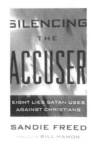
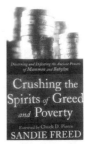

The Jezebel Yoke: Breaking Free from Bondage and Deception

Since the Garden of Eden, God's children have let the Deceiver seduce them away from their rightful blessings and, as a result, their true identities. Most are not even aware they are being deceived. With her trademark boldness and warmth, respected spiritual warfare expert Sandie Freed exposes spirits of deception--including Jezebel, Belial, Ahab, and more--and the tactics these demonic entities use to steal Christians' spiritual birthright. She also provides clarity and insight into the many ways believers are deceived and offers keys to inviting God's blessing. By showing readers how to shift back into their divine destinies, Sandie once again delivers a book that will set believers down the road to freedom.

ISBN: 978-0800795252   Chosen Books

Silencing the Accuser: Eight Lies Satan Uses Against Christians

Many Christians are unaware of the lies Satan, the accuser, whispers in their ears. Not only does he accuse believers, but he deceives them concerning their relationships with God and also their identities. Using the Old Testament story of Job, author Sandie Freed exposes our ancient enemy and the multiple ways he manipulates believers. With her trademark transparency and warmth, Freed encourages those struggling with a sense of hopelessness, a negative self-image, or a season of attacks--to name just three. She shows readers how to root out and overcome the negative thoughts the accuser plants, arming them with battle-tested prayer strategies to silence him and his deadly whisperings forever.

ISBN: 978-0800795108   Chosen Books

Crushing the Spirits of Greed and Poverty

This book provides a fresh perspective on the biblical messages of "Where your treasure is, there your heart will be also" and "The love of money is a root of all kinds of evil." Sandie Freed reveals the real root of money problems. With insight and wisdom, Freed exposes the seductive power of mammon. She arms readers to fight these strongholds with the powerful Word of God and real life, personal examples of victory as she shows them how to break their bondages to wealth, riches, status, and anxiety over finances. Not a book on how to create a budget, make money, or invest wisely, this release empowers readers to seek God's wisdom and favor concerning wealth. Only then can believers find financial and spiritual freedom.

ISBN: 978-0800794903   Chosen Books

Sandie Freed Books

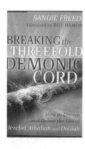  

Breaking the Threefold Demonic Cord

God has a divine plan to release his people from the curse of desolation and barrenness. Satan also has a strategy, however, which is to lock us to our past. He uses a three-fold cord of strongholds that seek to destroy us from victorious Christian living. But by exposing the plans of the enemy, God's people can be released from barrenness and launched into expansion, growth, and multiplication. Sandie Freed takes readers through a close study of each of these demonic forces in order to prepare them to break the threefold demonic cord. Conducting a biblical exploration of the everyday tactics of each spirit, Freed lays bare their strategies and helps readers defeat them through prayer.

ISBN: 978-0800794361   Chosen Books

Destiny Thieves

God has a plan for every one of his children. But there are powers working against this plan that attempt to subvert the destiny of believers. Just as Adam and Eve were seduced into sin by the serpent, Christians today still experience these destructive powers that threaten to steal their divine destiny. In this book, Sandie Freed shares the story of her own struggle, as well as many biblical accounts of the struggles of God's people, with the demonically inspired obstacles that stand in the way of breakthrough. This liberating book shows readers the tactics Satan uses against believers, identifies particular seducing spirits, and charges believers with a new level of faith to go forward and claim the victorious life God has planned for them.

ISBN: 978-0800794200   Chosen Books

Heaven's Voice

Do you want to hear from Heaven? Of course you do! That's why this book is another must read by Sandie Freed. Known for her humor in sharing her life experiences and her prophetic insight, Sandie has once again penned her revelation to mobilize the Church into victory. Heaven has a distinctive language and the Lord desires that we hear the sound of Heaven and shift into our future. This book is packed full of revelation to empower you to hear and understand how God is speaking today through sounds. Topics include: how to have spiritual ears, how to recognize the sound of war, and how to shift as a Third Day church.

ISBN: 978-0939868520   Kingdom Word Publishers

Watch Sandie Freed on

Author Interviews

Author Teachings

Author Book Synoposis

CONTACT US

SandieFreed.com

T: 817.284.5966

zionministries1@
sbcglobal.net

Sandie Freed Blog

Catch Sandie's
latest blog online at:
www.SandieFreed.com.

Filled with Revelation
& Insight to
help you on your journey.

Join Dr. Sandie's Mailing List

TODAY!!